Die Fahne Hoch: Three Biographies of Horst Wessel

DIE FAHNE HOCH

THREE BIOGRAPHIES OF HORST WESSEL

Horst Wessel: Life and Death
By Erwin Reitmann

SA Sturmführer Horst Wessel: A Portrait of a Life of Sacrifice
By Fritz Daum

Horst Wessel: Through Storm and Struggle to Immortality
By Max Kullak

TRANSLATED BY KLOKKE VAN AELST

ANTELOPE HILL PUBLISHING

First printing 2022.

The original content of these works is in the public domain. Three separate works have been translated and combined into this collection:

1. *Horst Wessel: Life and Death* by Erwin Reitmann, originally published in German as *Horst Wessel—Leben und Sterben* by Traditions-Verlag Kolf & Co., Berlin, 1933.
2. *SA Sturmführer Horst Wessel: A Portrait of a Life of Sacrifice* by Fritz Daum, originally published in German as *SA.-Sturmführer Horst Wessel—Ein Lebensbild von Opfertreue* by Enßlin & Laiblins Verlagsbuchhandlung, Reutlingen, 1933.
3. *Horst Wessel: Through Storm and Struggle to Immortality* by Max Kullak, originally published in German as *Horst Wessel—Durch Sturm und Kampf zur Unsterblichkeit* by Langenfalza, Verlag von Julius Beltz, Berlin and Leipzig, 1934.

Translated by Klokke van Aelst, 2022.

Cover design by Swifty. Painting by Karl Mühlmeister appeared in *SA.-Sturmführer Horst Wessel—Ein Lebensbild von Opfertreue.*

Edited by Tom Simpson.
Formatted by Margaret Bauer.

Antelope Hill Publishing
antelopehillpublishing.com

Paperback ISBN-13: 978-1-956887-20-4
EPUB ISBN-13: 978-1-956887-21-1

CONTENTS

SA *Sturmführer* Horst Wessel: A Portrait of a Life of Sacrifice

Horst Wessel: Through Storm and Struggle to Immortality

INTRODUCTION

Horst Wessel: a man whose name is still known today, more than ninety years after his passing. He died a martyr for National Socialism, as Dr. Joseph Goebbels described him, and became the face of an entire organization and the symbol of a movement the likes of which the world had never witnessed before. Although the Berlin *Sturmführer* enjoyed only local fame during his lifetime, after his death his name became the common knowledge of every German. Streets, squares, hospitals, and monuments were devoted to him. One of his songs, known as the *"Horst-Wessel-Lied,"* would even become the party anthem of the NSDAP.

Horst Wessel: an interesting figure to examine both from a historical as well as a meta-political point of view. One would be surprised that, despite his fame, practically no biographical texts were written about him after the Second World War. Daniel Siemens seems to be the only exception in this regard. In his book, *Horst Wessel: Tod und Verklärung eines Nationalsozialisten*, originally published in Germany in 2009 and translated in 2013 under the title *The Making of a Nazi Hero—The Murder and Myth of Horst Wessel*, he presents the most complete biographical account of the young man to date. When it comes to quality translations of original German biographies published in the years after Wessel's death, however, one could only look in vain—until now. This compendium brings together three works from the 1930s, translated for the first time for an English-speaking audience:

1. *Horst Wessel—Leben und Sterben* by Erwin Reitmann, originally published in 1933 by Traditions-Verlag Kolf & Co. in Berlin.

2. *SA.-Sturmführer Horst Wessel—Ein Lebensbild von Opfertreue* by Fritz Daum, originally published in 1933 by Enßlin & Laiblins Verlagsbuchhandlung in Reutlingen.

3. *Horst Wessel—Durch Sturm und Kampf zur Unsterblichkeit* by Max

Kullak, originally published in 1934 by Langenfalza, Verlag von Julius Beltz in Berlin and Leipzig.

Erwin Reitmann was a fellow combatant of Horst Wessel. One can therefore assume that he knew Wessel very well and thus knew what he was writing about. Nevertheless, Reitmann's biography feels mostly like propaganda, which is to say, that it feels like the least-subtle propaganda compared to the other two works. This is somewhat ironic when one reads the purpose of the book on the first page: "It is intended to paint a clear and unembellished picture of the unique personality of Horst Wessel."

Fritz Daum's biography seems to be the most complete. It is also by far the longest of the three and, like Reitmann's, the amount of propagandism is very high, almost equaling the latter. The subtitle of this book shows that the specific target audience was the German youth. However, this does not mean that the language used is childish in any way. Daum tries to set as perfect an example as possible for the young readers, in which he succeeds by means of the narrative style of the book.

Max Kullak brings us the shortest book of the three. Like Erwin Reitmann, Kullak was a member of the SA, as shown by the dedication at the beginning of the book. Whether he was acquainted with Wessel is not known. Despite the brevity of this biography, the author manages to give a unique view on several events. As an additional bonus many songs that are included in this book. In the translation of both this and the other two books, the original German lyrics have been preserved alongside the English translation. Not providing the original lyrics would not do justice to the splendor of the German language and it would deprive the reader of the chance to read these verses as they were once sung in real life.

Translating three books that describe the life of one and the same person—although in different ways—has some advantages. Each author places different touches in his own work. Where one book only mentions a person or an event by name, for example, the other book expands on it at length. For example, Reitmann mentions the recruitment drive to Pasewalk in a single sentence, whereas Daum and Kullak each devote a separate chapter to it. Conversely, Kullak pays little attention to the death of Werner Wessel, Horst's younger brother, while Reitmann and certainly Daum successfully use the boy's death to portray Horst as a true hero. The same can be said of

Erna Jänicke, Horst's alleged girlfriend, whom he saved from the hands of the Red Front.[1] Reitmann mentions her by name only once and Kullak does not even mention her at all. In Daum's case, on the other hand, Jänicke actually has an important supporting role. A possible explanation for the omission of the existence of this lady will be discussed below. Numerous other examples can be given besides these, including the incidents involving the shawm band and the entry into the Fischerkietz.

A second advantage can be directly linked to this. By reading the three parts of this compendium side-by-side, the reader not only obtains a picture of the life of Horst Wessel himself, but also, to a certain extent, a picture of Horst's family and friends. For example, both Kullak and Daum tell the story of *Sturmführer* Albert Sprengel and how he came to be nicknamed "Barrikadenalbert." Werner and Inge Wessel, Richard Fiedler, and Dr. Joseph Goebbels are also recurring characters.

Because these three books deal with a specific time and place, terms and names are used which are not a part of today's general knowledge. Especially for a non-German speaking audience, names like Reichsbanner, Corps Normannia, and the Bismarck League, to name a few, will sound strange. However, from explicit and implicit explanations present in the books, the reader will be able to determine the meaning and significance of these organizations. Footnotes have been added to give context and to enhance the experience of the reader.

In a more general way, the reader also gets a good idea of what life in Berlin was like in the 1920s. Propaganda trips to the villages around Berlin, political speeches in smoke-filled pubs and conference halls, large-scale street and bar fights between individuals of various political factions, evenings filled with the singing of new storm songs, nights in prison filled with the singing of those same storm songs, bloody faces, broken bones, bruised ribs and, yes, bullet holes; it was all part of the daily life of many young people in those days.

This brings us to a third advantage. By placing three different reports side-by-side and reading them carefully, some interesting

---

[1] The Red Front Fighter's League (shortened to the Red Front) was a paramilitary organization affiliated with the Communist Party of Germany in the Weimar Republic. In German, the group's full name is *Roter Frontkämpferbund*, which was also abbreviated as RFB.

discrepancies emerge. The most striking difference is found in the last moments before the attempt on Horst Wessel's life. In Kullak we read that Wessel, when he hears knocking on the door exclaims, "Come in, Albert." In Reitmann's case we read another name: "Come in, Richard." The fact is that we do not know which name he called out. However, both names are possibilities since both were good comrades of Wessel. After all, Albert here refers to Albert Sprengel and Richard to Richard Fiedler. In another place we read about the limited funeral procession at Horst Wessel's funeral. Reitmann writes that ten wagons were allowed to follow the hearse. In the case of Kullak and Daum, there were only seven.

The above discrepancies are ultimately only minor details. However, they make it clear that the reader should not necessarily believe every detail in these books. This is especially true for every sentence that is placed between quotation marks. It seems almost impossible that the three authors knew exactly what Wessel said during his conversations as a child. Equally impossible seem the lively conversations with the nurse after the assault on his life that Reitmann and Daum write about. These doubts are reinforced by the official description of his injuries: his tongue, uvula, and palate would have been largely blown away by the impact of the bullet. Elsewhere we read about *Mensur*, a ritual fencing match customary in certain student associations in the German regions. According to Daum, Wessel would have trained this with his left arm after hurting his right arm. If we are to believe Walter Reinhart, a fellow Corps member of Wessel's, Horst would have been able to do anything but master the art, even after many training sessions. The author of this introduction, having held a *Mensur* sword—a *Mensurschläger*—in his hands on several occasions in Germany, can also confirm that this is not something that can be mastered easily, let alone with the left arm. Finally, figures also seem somewhat embellished. Thousands are said to have attended the funerals of both Horst and Werner. Is it possible? Yes. Is it credible? A little less so.

Regarding quotations attributed to Horst Wessel, there are also several exact similarities between the different books. The best example is again found in Kullak and Reitmann. When Horst is present at a meeting of the Social Democratic Party, he says, according to both authors, "*Ich bin zwar noch sehr jung, aber sehen Sie, gerade die Jugend hat ja letzten Endes unter den heutigen Zuständen am meisten zu leiden.*"[2] Did both authors have access to the same source? Did Kullak, who published his book in 1934, have access to the work of Reitmann, whose book had appeared one year prior? We have no way of knowing. One should not forget that a biography by Hanns Heinz Ewers was also published in 1932. The same question can be asked: did Kullak, Reitmann and Daum have access to Ewers' work? For the time being, an English translation of this last book is still lacking; an answer to this last question is therefore also pending.

Finally, attention can be drawn to the details that the authors leave out, whether intentionally or not. For example, we read that Wessel gave up his law studies to become a worker. In reality, he left university after repeatedly getting bad grades. Then, there is the elephant in the room: Erna Jänicke. Above it was mentioned that Kullak does not mention this lady and that Reitmann mentions her only once. This is somewhat bizarre, given that Jänicke was present in the apartment at the time of the assault. She is mentioned frequently in Daum's book, and both he and Reitmann refer to her as the girl who was saved by Horst from the clutches of communism. What all three authors forget to mention is that Jänicke was a former prostitute. Daum, however, seems to make the allusion, albeit very subtly.

The communist magazines went one step further and called Wessel her pimp, murdered because he had stolen her from the pimp Ali Höhler, who is better known as Wessel's murderer. That this is not explicitly written down should not, of course, be surprising. It would merely give a bad image: a pimp as a role model for the new youth. That Wessel was Jänicke's pimp is anything but an established fact, as corroborated by the court testimonies by both Jänicke and Höhler. They only knew each other by name, and further relations did not exist.

It is by no means the intention here to depict Horst Wessel as a scoundrel, nor to label the three authors as liars. Let it be clear that these three books are propaganda. The boundary between biography and hagiography is not absolute in this case. Also, the line between fantasy and reality is not always clear. However, this does not take away from the fact that Horst Wessel did achieve certain things as a

---

[2] "I'm still very young, but you see, it's the youth who suffer the most from today's conditions."

Sturmführer. The story of the shawm band is a good example. From higher-up, the establishment of a band was forbidden. Wessel was the first to establish one anyway, with great success in the field of propaganda as a result. The fact that Wessel was the most requested speaker for speeches after *Gauleiter* Joseph Goebbels, as both Reitmann and Kullak attest, also corresponds with reality. And although he did not write the melody himself, the *"Horst-Wessel-Lied"* is one of his creations: a creation that is still known almost a century later.

Each of these books contributes to the myth of Horst Wessel: a young man, inspired by the ideals of the Führer, Adolf Hitler, and determined to put them into practice. In certain respects, Hitler and Wessel have some things in common. Both lost their father at a very young age, and both grew up in relatively turbulent times. However, this is also where the biggest difference between them lies. Horst Wessel, the son of a pastor, may have grown up in Weimar Germany, but the years of learning and suffering that the Führer endured in Vienna are foreign to him, not to mention the war years at the battlefront in Flanders. A leader born from among the people Wessel was not. The three authors know this and act appropriately to make Wessel the hero he needed to be. The focus is not on his experiences as a proletarian, as is the case for Hitler in Mein Kampf, but on his experiences as a well-to-do citizen in relation to the proletariat. Wessel is given a double task: he first had to become one of the people before uniting them.

Answering the question of who Horst Wessel was as a person is a research question for historians. From a meta-political perspective, this question is less relevant. Here it is not Horst Wessel as a person, but Horst Wessel as an idea that is of importance. It is unimportant which facts correspond to reality and which facts were embellished for propagandistic purposes. It is about an idea, an archetype. The new youth was in need of an example in the fight for a new Germany. Young, heroic, determined, resilient, faithful to the ideals; a true National Socialist. This is the role model the youth needed, and this role model bears the name Horst Wessel.

Klokke van Aelst
April 20th, 2022

HORST WESSEL: LIFE AND DEATH

ERWIN REITMANN

This book is intended to help faithfully preserve the memory of the martyr of the National Socialist Freedom Movement.

It is intended to paint a clear and unembellished picture of the unique personality of Horst Wessel. And above all, it should allow the greatness and purity of our worldview to be measured by the life, struggles, and death of the dead hero.

PREFACE

As an old comrade-in-arms of Horst Wessel, I felt called upon and obliged to erect a memorial stone in this form to my dead comrade, the hero of the National Socialist movement.

I speak here as one of the many who were allowed to fight for Germany's liberation in Horst Wessel's storm. These leaves are intended to express the gratitude of thousands of SA men who today faithfully guard the name and legacy of this great martyr.

May this book be a source of spiritual strength for the reader, from which he can draw when his strength begins to fade in the fight for Germany.

Erwin Reitmann
Berlin, July 1932

HORST WESSEL: A PORTRAIT OF HIS LIFE

Kamerad Wessel
Hanz Flut

Kamerad Wessel, wir trauern um dich . . .
Unsere Augen verlernten das Weinen;
Unsere Augen wollten Versteinen,
Da uns das Leuchten der deinen verblich—
Kamerad Wessel, wir trauern um dich!

Kamerad Wessel, wir ehren dich . . .
Tief zur Erde die Fahnen wir senken;
Hoch nach Walhall die Blicke wir lenken,
Schaudernd, als wenn ein Adler entwich—
Kamerad Wessel, wir ehren dich!

Kamerad Wessel, wir denken an dich . . .
Wenn für Deutschlands Zukunft wir streiten,
Soll dein heldischer Geist uns begleiten
Brausend wie Lenzwind, der wild uns umstrich—
Kamerad Wessel, wir denken an dich!

Kamerad Wessel, wir rächen dich . . .
Schwelend genährt von Elend und Schmerzen;
Bricht einst der Haß aus gemarterten Herzen,
Lodernde Flamme, die nimmer verblich—
Kamerad Wessel, wir rächen dich!

Comrade Wessel
Hanz Flut

Comrade Wessel, we mourn you . . .
Our eyes have forgotten how to cry;
Our eyes wanted to fade away,
As we lost the glow of yours—
Comrade Wessel, we mourn you!

Comrade Wessel, we honor you . . .
Low to the ground we lower our flags;
High to Valhalla our gazes we direct,
Shivering as if an eagle had taken flight -
Comrade Wessel, we honor you!

Comrade Wessel, we think of you . . .
When we fight for Germany's future
Let your heroic spirit accompany us
As fierce as the breeze that blew around us—
Comrade Wessel, we think of you!

Comrade Wessel, we will avenge you . . .
Smoldering, nourished by misery and pain;
Once hatred breaks out of tortured hearts,
A blazing flame that never faded away
Comrade Wessel, we avenge you!

"Germany must live, even if we must die!"

In the present age of decline of all moral values, of flattening of character and dulling of the spirit, which has spread particularly strongly among young people thanks to a certain system, the name of Horst Wessel illuminates the dark present like a ray of light. Horst Wessel's life and death must serve as a beacon to the world around us. Horst Wessel—student and worker! The new German man who dedicated his whole life to the fight for freedom.

"Nothing for myself—everything for Germany" was not just a phrase for him. He always proved that he was serious about it.

Horst Wessel's holy blood-sacrifice was a seed on the thorny path to German freedom that has blossomed in many ways. Many have gone before him on the blood-soaked path, and many, many, will follow him.

The great, young deceased showed thousands of despairing fellow Germans that there are still ideals for which German people lay down their lives. Under the radiant swastika flags a spiritual type has formed, the most beautiful and glorious personification of which is Horst Wessel.

In the middle of the Westphalian countryside by the mighty Teutoburg Forest, Horst Wessel was born in Bielefeld on October 9th, 1907 as the son of the pastor Dr. Ludwig Wessel. He was the first sprout to come out of a happy marriage. Westphalia has tough soil and equally tough people. Westphalians are people rooted in the soil, as Hermann Löns described them.

Until his sixth year, little Horst spent an untroubled youth in Mülheim upon the Ruhr, in the land of coal mines and pits. His father worked here as a pastor, but was called to the famous St. Nikolai Church in Berlin in 1913, from whose chapel the hymn writer Paul Gerhardt had once preached.

Close to the St. Nikolai Church, on the border of Old Berlin and the busy hustle and bustle of the city center, lies the Jüdenstraße.[3] Horst spent his youth here in house number 51/52. The adjoining hidden streets and alleys always offered the best opportunity for cheerful play. Many a time he would have heard the beautiful chimes of the parochial church in the side street, which trembled through the quiet alleys and streets every half hour.

When the World War broke out in 1914, his father joined the German army as its first volunteer chaplain. As a government priest, he served the Fatherland first in Belgium, then in Kaunas at the headquarters of Field Marshal von Hindenburg.

Horst had a sister named Ingeborg and a brother named Werner. Horst Wessel and his brother Werner were brothers through thick and thin. They could not be separated from each other. One did not leave the other. Although the two brothers got along well, they were very different in character. Werner Wessel, who in contrast to Horst was more of a romantic, tried to emulate his brother in every way.

---

[3] Jewish Street

After enjoying traveling for a long time and being completely devoted to the subject, he later found his way to National Socialism and exchanged his traveling coat for the brown uniform.

Horst also enjoyed hiking at first, but very early on he became involved in politics. He was a level-headed, realistic thinker who was well ahead for his age. At school he was the "hero" of the class and, as his great talent allowed him to follow along with ease, he could get away with jokes that made the whole class laugh. He was the ringleader who cooked up many a prank with his classmates. Once the teacher gave the pupils the task of writing down their political opinion in an essay. Since the matter could be done anonymously, Horst was on-board in no time and wrote an essay that pleased the teacher to no end.

Horst Wessel attended the Humanist Gymnasium, graduated from high school at the age of eighteen and studied law. He joined the Kösener Corps Normannia. After some time, he went to Vienna and became a member of the Alemannia Corps there. It was then that Horst's student days had begun, but not those preoccupied with beer and wine. He had decided on a different worldview. As a young man he had already joined the political front—also a sign of the spiritual need of our youth, which thirsts for freedom like no other generation has.

Horst Wessel's tremendous temperament, his love for his father-land, and his ardent idealism broke the shackles of a rich bourgeois life. He did not find what he was looking for in the *Bismarckbund*,[4] of which he was a member at first. But even then, as later on, it became clear that, like a magnet, he attracted the best forces to himself and immediately became the leader and spokesman of the opposition. He instinctively realized that the *Bismarckbund* was not an association of revolutionary youth. The leadership had grown old, and the lack of a worldview meant that the best people soon left. Horst joined because he knew of no better association. After some time, however, he found his way to the Wiking, and here he believed he had found the right thing. He was completely committed to the cause. He worked day and night. Everywhere he campaigned and pushed forward. He himself once wrote, "School and home fell into insignificance in

---

[4] The *Bismarckbund* was the youth branch of the German National People's Party in the Weimar Republic

comparison [to politics]."

The struggle for the political ideal was more important to him than anything else. His innate talent as a leader soon put him in a leading position in this military association as well. He could not do enough for his people. What he demanded of himself as a matter of principle, he believed he could also demand of others. It was simply incomprehensible to him how people did not give it their all. This is the only way to understand what he once wrote: "As soon as I had a break, mostly during the holidays, the comradeship also broke down completely. You had to work on people continuously, otherwise they would soon give up. Strange, really, because in and of itself an idea that doesn't drive even the followers to work together is worth nothing."

Through the Wiking, Horst also joined the Black *Reichswehr* and received a brief military training.[5] His mother tells of how Horst left one day and she never heard from him again. After six weeks, she finally received the news from her son that he had been trained in the Black *Reichswehr*—instead of enjoying the summer holiday.

Even in moments like these, Horst Wessel's entrepreneurial spirit and boldness were evident.

His affiliation with the Wiking, the so-called Organization Consul (O.C.), did not last too long.

All the idealism and self-sacrifice he had mustered for this military organization had been uselessly squandered. The surrender of Ehrhardt had left him, like so many other comrades, severely disappointed and embittered. Horst withdrew from politics, but could not bear to stand on the sidelines in the fight for Germany's rebirth for long.

In the autumn of 1926 Horst joined the National Socialists, not out of recognition, but out of disappointment, as he himself wrote. Here he finally found what he had longed for all these years and what he had aspired to with all his heart: a greater ideal.

With a restless soul, he had previously been wandering between worlds. Now he had finally found the path to inner satisfaction. He immersed himself with all thoroughness in the teachings of the National Socialist worldview and thoroughly re-educated himself in

---

[5] Black *Reichswehr* was the name given to different paramilitary groups which were supported by the German *Reichswehr* (armed forces) in the Weimar Republic.

all fields. He had always been an ardent nationalist, but now he also became a socialist, without which there can be no genuine nationalism. Therefore, Horst became a socialist as much out of instinct as out of reason! The love for his impoverished fellow Germans—social justice at any price—had long been glowing in his breast as a warning spark that never went out. The realization now kindled this spark into a soaring flame. Later, as a speaker and *Sturmführer*, one could often enough observe his passionate, ruthless, advocacy for the oppressed, downtrodden workers. It was characteristic that he felt most at ease in the company of modest people. For God's sake, no arrogance! How he hated those elements of the bourgeoisie who looked down on the workers in their overalls. He confronted these guilt-ridden pests with bitter mockery and sublime irony. It is also thanks to Horst Wessel's radical attitude that he later, as a *Sturmführer*, pulled so many people out of the Marxist front.

Wessel's first activity within the party began in the SA, when he went to Pasewalk and Kottbus. In January of 1928 he went to Vienna and stayed there until July. The Berlin District Leader, Dr. Goebbels, gave him the task of studying the structure and working methods of the Hitler Youth in Vienna. This activity proved immensely beneficial. He often told his co-workers that he had learned a great deal from the Vienna Hitler Youth, which he then applied to the SA. When he returned to Berlin from Vienna, he first took over the post of head of a street cell in the Alexanderplatz section. Here he did valuable groundwork. He formed a good corps of functionaries through evening training sessions.

One evening Horst Wessel found himself standing at the lectern in the meeting hall and spoke. Horst had suddenly become a speaker. How much more he could gain from this activity! He must have restored the faith in Germany of hundreds, even thousands, of people during his many meetings. Who was more suited to be a speaker than he, with his passion, his idealism, his quick wit, and his oratory skills? Soon word spread everywhere. He was requested in Berlin and the Brandenburg region. He was the second-busiest speaker after Dr. Goebbels. It was a tactic of Horst Wessel's to declare right at the beginning of his speech: "I may still be very young, but you see, it is precisely the youth who ultimately have to suffer most innocently from today's state of affairs." With this tactic, he took the wind out of the sails of old, crusty opponents right from the start.

In the meantime, Horst Wessel's great abilities had been discovered and he was now the center of attention. He was offered the post of *Sturmführer* on several occasions. Too busy with his work as a speaker, he declined several times. But when he was called to join Troop 34 in Friedrichshain on May 1st, 1929, he accepted and in no time at all built up a storm in this district of strong communist resistance that had no equal in Berlin.

Storm 5 soon achieved a certain notoriety. "Respected by friends; feared by the enemy" very quickly became a reality. Day and night Horst Wessel was on the move, neglecting all else. The storm grew from day to day in an almost frightening way. How did this happen? Horst Wessel had soon realized that there were still a great many idealists in the Marxist camp, and his whole struggle was directed towards winning over these valuable forces. It is to Horst Wessel's great credit that he began the struggle for one of Berlin's communist strongholds, the eastern part of Berlin, with a death-defying, pro-portionally small group. The methods and the nature of the struggle were ultimately decisive. The boldness with which he drove the movement forward at first caused a paralyzing astonishment in his opponents, which then very soon gave way to bloodthirsty revenge. All the plans of the great struggle were organically underpinned. We worked according to a certain system. First, we provoked the enemy through marches and similar actions. In this way we achieved an engagement from the local opponent with us, which they did well enough. Then it was not long before the first people from the Red Front appeared at our rallies. A not insignificant number of them did not come out of recognition, but were attracted by the personality of Horst Wessel. Here the process of transformation orchestrated by Horst Wessel started. Since the Führer usually always gathers people of good character around him, it is not surprising that a crowd of bold people soon gathered around Wessel. They came from all quarters and wanted to join in. Like a magnet, Wessel drew people to him. Through struggle, leader and followers were bound together ever more tightly. A wonderful fighting community developed. The people went through fire for their Horst, and he himself was attached to his people with all of his heart. Whenever Horst Wessel was together with his comrades, he made use of their language and expressions to the utmost. The whole appearance immediately revealed the outstanding leader, but not the academic! It was no wonder that it was precisely the humblest people from the proletarian class who felt attracted to him! They talked to him as if he were their best friend, and yet no one dared to challenge his authority. That Horst was the leader was so self-evident to everyone, it simply had to be, and everyone was proud of their leader. It is easy to understand that there were not too many intellectual know-it-alls in this circle.

Wessel detested narrow-mindedness; modesty and straight-forwardness suited him. He also did not fail to dress well. He preferred to wear bear boots, breeches, and a waistcoat.

Horst had a healthy sense of humor, and we were to experience his brightness and quick wit many more times in the future.

You could have taken him for a real Berliner by the whole of his character and behavior. Horst didn't let anything happen to his comrades, and if he was in the right, he defended his position relentlessly to the highest degree.

In order to fully understand the working class, in order to connect with it more and more, he worked as a student at a construction site. Here he got to know the soul of the worker down to the deepest depths, but here he also had to put up with the terror and nastiness of the Marxists. Being a student, Horst was always in a position to lead a comfortable life, and yet he did not. He was not afraid to swing a hammer, carry stones, or shovel sand like they did. Socialism, the love for the fellow countrymen, was deeply ingrained in him. He tried to get closer and closer to his comrades. He renounced all material goods. He proved to them that he was their leader, but as a human being he lived just as frugally as they did.

Entirely on his own, he made his way through life.

Horst had dearly earned the trust of his comrades. Even the lowest-ranking SA member had the greatest trust in him. Only in this way was it possible for Wessel to do the most fantastic, daring things with his comrades. He could rely on his troops completely. Horst was the type of political soldier, a role model for his people in the truest sense of the word. He often undertook the most daring actions with his storm. On the storm evening meetings, however, he tried with all of his might to implant the teachings of National Socialism in the hearts of his people.

His talent as a speaker and his knowledge served him well here. These were not dull evenings of instruction, for the way Horst educated his people to become National Socialists kept everyone engaged.

Due to the constant growth of the storm, which some comrades observed with increasing concern, we eventually had to hold the storm evening meetings in conference venues. In time, however, the constant influx from the Marxist camp also brought in subversive elements who tried to sow discord between the leader and the members. The enemy had instinctively recognized Horst Wessel's dangerousness and left no stone unturned to eliminate him.

How bitterly he must have suffered from the subsequent quarrels, how it must have hurt him, the great idealist, that members of his own ranks rose up against him and began to undermine his achievements, which he had built up with so much love and relentless labor.

He could truly have lived a quiet life. The whole world lay open to him. His mother wanted him to go on a vacation to visit his two uncles living in South America after he had passed his final exams. Horst decided against it. The bond that had wrapped itself around him and his comrades was now too tight to let him go.

He was offered the post of *Oberführer* in Mecklenburg, but he declined it. The struggle for Berlin, for the red East Berlin: that was his mission.

His captivating songs, which are now sung everywhere by the awakened nation, came into being. How his big eyes gleamed when he was able to present his comrades with a new song. When he sang the song *"Die Fahne Hoch"* for the first time at the storm evening meeting,[6] probably none of his comrades-in-arms believed that he had helped create a song which today has become the liberation song of millions of Germans. The song *"Die Fahne Hoch"* bears witness to Horst Wessel's genuine spirit, and it speaks of courage, pride, resistance, faith, and hope. An awakened Germany sings the song with joy and pain; it resounds equally passionately in city and country.

The song has long since become immortal. Future generations will be reminded of the time of Germany's greatest shame, against which one of the most glorious freedom movements ran. But above all, it will recall the great blood-sacrifices that a flourishing, idealistic youth made for their fatherland.

---

[6] "Raise the Flag"

Who in Germany today does not know the "Horst Wessel Song"? Even in the "*Hohe Haus*," the *Reichstag*, this glorious song resounded when a hundred and seven National Socialists left the room in February of 1931 to protest against the repressive policies of the Brüning government. No meeting, no rally, no gathering of National Socialists ends before the "Horst Wessel Song" has been sung.

How proud Horst Wessel was at that time when he could announce that the song had already been requested by so and so many SA formations from all over the Reich. Even at that time we saw that the song was triumphantly spreading through Germany at lightning speed. It was as though everyone had been awaiting this song. Many a time Horst sat down at the piano at the storm evening meetings and performed a new song he had written for his comrades. Storm 5 always provided new songs, which were then carried on by the others. The evening meetings always began with a song and also ended that way. Horst always gave his storm new songs.

He brought the "*Wiener Jungarbeiterlied*" to Berlin, where it quickly became popular.[7]

The storm evening meeting was a moment of joy, when all the new thoughts and plans he had accumulated over the course of a week were shared with his comrades. Here he was in a circle of people who understood and admired him, here he came out of his shell and always made an effort to give it his all.

How jubilant everyone was when Horst announced one day that we were going to buy a shawm band. We were still a little in disbelief, but very quickly we owned one.

Despite his great masculine maturity, he had a heart like a child. He was attached to his mother and siblings with the deepest love.

But as harmonious as Wessel's family life was, National Socialism exerted too much power. The quiet tranquility and harmony were soon destroyed. The duty to serve their fatherland tore the Wessel sons away from their mother. First National Socialism took Horst Wessel, but soon his mother also had to give her second son Werner.

Their mother once said in a conversation, "I had my sons completely under control; just one wink of the eye was enough, but National Socialism was stronger than I was."

---

[7] The "Viennese Young Workers' Song"

Werner Wessel was serving in Storm 1 at the time when Horst was expanding his storm. The two brothers went on marches together in the same unit. Even though Werner Wessel did not have the energy and leadership talent of his brother, he soon became indispensable to his storm. He also gave his storm a number of very beautiful songs, which soon became common property throughout the Berlin SA.

On December 23rd, 1929, Werner Wessel had an accident while out snowshoeing. The snowshoeing group of the Berlin National Socialists was on a trip to the Giant Mountains. They got caught in a terrible snowstorm that drove off several people from the group, including Werner Wessel. They tried in vain to make their way to the rescue hut, but the blizzard prevented all vision. Werner Wessel and the other comrades, already completely exhausted, sat down to rest. That was their downfall, for sleep overtook them and the white death claimed four blooming lives as its victims. The rescue teams set out too late; they could only recover the bodies.

On the same day, Horst Wessel paid his last respects to the murdered National Socialist Fischer with his storm. Who knew that such a terrible thing had happened at the same time? The next day, the newspapers carried the news throughout the entire Reich. The bodies of the victims were laid out in the Wang church. Werner Wessel's mother wanted her son to be buried next to her husband's final resting place in the Nikolai cemetery.

The transport of the deceased by rail was delayed because of the holidays. So Horst decided to take his brother to Berlin by truck. He got behind the wheel himself and drove off with a companion.

It was a sad journey through the Silesian districts. He was on the road day and night. Overtired, he set off on the journey homeward, the coffin with the body of his brother and the two other victims from Berlin behind him in the covered carriage. Exhausted, he fell asleep on the road in the middle of the night and did not wake up until late in the morning.

Werner was laid out in his parents' home. On December 28th, he was laid to rest and thousands of National Socialists paid their last respects to the young deceased. They had carried him to the grave like a prince. When the coffin, covered with the swastika flag, was lowered into the grave, the song of the "*Gute Kamerad*" rang out.

Torches were flickering back and forth, and it was late in the evening when the last comrades took leave of Werner Wessel's remains.

When Storm 5 marched through the Jüdenstraße after the funeral and passed by Wessel's house, Horst stood at the window and silently saluted his beloved storm with his arm raised. Here was shown the symbol of a community in hardship and death.

After a long time, Horst took part in the storm evening meetings again, but it was apparent immediately that he made a crestfallen, almost broken-down impression. The usual sparkle in his eyes had disappeared, no more jokes came from his lips, and a deep sadness lurked in his being. It seemed as if he had suddenly alienated himself from his people. The death of his brother had been a heavy blow to his heart, and melancholy seemed to rule over him completely. I had never seen Horst quite happy since then; he had suddenly become another person.

All this hardship had put him on the sickbed. Spies and traitors believed that their hour had come. The storm evening meetings no longer presented the usual picture; a cold, sober tone set in. The subordinate leaders who now stepped in were at first unable to cope with the situation. Dark forces began to undermine the leader, and when they started to move against him in secret, they failed because of the cohesion of the storm.

Now Horst Wessel's indispensability became apparent. He was the sole master of this great storm; without him the storm was a ship without a captain.

The storm evening meetings lost their charm, everyone hoped that Horst would soon reappear, and then that Storm 5 would once again become what it had been for so long: the much-feared elite storm of the Berlin SA.

But things were to turn out differently. It was January 14th, 1930, when all the evening papers in Berlin announced in big letters: "Assassination attempt on a National Socialist student!" and ran pictures of Horst Wessel. People read hurriedly, halting, stumbling, looking, and staring over and over again. We all refused to believe it; it seemed almost incomprehensible to us, and yet we had to believe it. It was a fact, a harsh fact. Comrades who belonged to Horst Wessel's inner circle had feared this for a long time and left no stone unturned to keep him out of the greatest danger. Communist criminals were constantly on his trail and hunted him down like a wounded animal. They were convinced that only Wessel was to blame for their red strongholds faltering, for the best activists leaving their front and now fighting against them under Wessel's command. Horst Wessel knew about this and acted accordingly. One day he lived here, then there, then he stayed with comrades for several days, then he lived somewhere as a lodger. His last place of residence was at Frankfurter Straße 62, opposite our last meeting place.

Here he was with Erna Jänicke, whom he had pulled out of communist circles. How else can this act, which brought him into conflict even with his relatives, be understood other than out of excessive, extreme idealism? A man of such moral strength as Horst Wessel could descend into the deepest depths of human life without damaging his soul. By virtue of his personality, he was able to transform people from the ground up.

Horst Wessel had rented a room from a certain Mrs. Salm. His landlady, a communist who was in contact with communist officials, wanted to "get rid" of her lodger. One evening, on January 14th, she went to a communist pub and told them that Horst Wessel was in her house. When the Communists heard this, they said, "Oh, that's the long-sought Wessel." Soon a select group of criminals was on its way, all individuals with criminal records, headed by the pimp and communist leader Ali Höhler and one Miss Cohn. The landlady Salm led the criminals into the apartment, while some of the gang stood guard downstairs.

There was a knock at Horst Wessel's door, and assuming it was his friend, *Sturmführer* Fiedler, he shouted "Come in, Richard," went to the door, and opened it.

At that moment he was fired upon. Hit in the mouth, Horst Wessel collapsed, covered in blood. When they tried to fetch a Jewish doctor, Horst, lying in his blood, refused. The murderers hastily ransacked the room for weapons and lists.

He was taken to the hospital in Friedrichshain. There, in terrible agony, both he and the entire National Socialist movement hoped for his recovery. When he was feeling a little better, his comrades were allowed to visit him; they passed his room and greeted him with their arm raised. Soon it seemed as if Horst Wessel could be saved, but then blood poisoning set in and brought all hope to an abrupt end. Horst was released from his agony on Sunday, February 23rd at 6:30 in the morning. No one wanted to believe it when the news of his death spread through Germany. Men and women wept at the young hero's death bier.

The whole of Germany comforted the mother who had been so sorely tried by fate.

On the first of March, a gray, dark day, the people of Berlin paid their last respects to the dead *Sturmführer*. The police forbade a funeral procession, and only ten cars were allowed to follow the procession. Even the covering of the coffin with the swastika flag was not allowed. We were forced to submit if we did not want to cause a great deal of bloodshed. Police with rubber truncheons in their hands accompanied the short procession. Black walls of people saluted the great martyr of the National Socialist movement in the streets for the last time.

Near the cemetery, the organized red subhumans had gathered and cheered, shouted and laughed as the procession passed. When they bombarded the funeral procession with rocks and tried to overturn the hearse, police had to intervene. Horst Wessel's last journey took place under such shameful, disgraceful circumstances. The funeral procession was attacked and beaten up everywhere on the way to the cemetery.

The Nikolai cemetery was crowded by thousands hours beforehand, so that it had to be closed off by the police. SA and student associations stood guard as the coffin, now covered with swastika flags and student caps, was carried to the grave by *Sturmführer* to the sound of the funeral march.

Behind the coffin walked the relatives and the storm of the deceased. When the coffin was lowered into the grave to the tune of the "*Gute Kamerad*," a hellish racket broke out behind the churchyard wall. There was laughing and whistling; stones flew over the wall, and the "*Internationale*" was roared. Unleashed sub-humanity did not even shy away from the majesty of death.

The two priests of St. Nikolai, the two representatives of the Corps Normannia and Corps Alemannia from Vienna, Hauptmann von Pfeffer, and Dr. Goebbels spoke at the grave. The latter drew a picture of the dearly departed. Men sobbed and women burst into tears. When the song of the deceased, "*Die Fahne Hoch*," roared across the cemetery on this gloomy evening, sung by thousands of people with death-stricken hearts, it overwhelmed everyone like an oath, and everyone vowed to turn Horst Wessel's song into reality.

Later that evening, men and women came to the grave, saluted the dead *Sturmführer* and laid flowers upon flowers on top of the fresh mound.

A guard had to stay behind to prevent the waste of humanity from disturbing the peace of the dead. Like dirty dogs, the people had to sneak home in the evening, for murder lurked in the dark streets.

Many comrades were still beaten up that evening.

Young people will be red with shame one day when they learn under what circumstances a German martyr was laid to rest.

Soon after the murder it became known where to look for the perpetrators. It was clear from the start that the masterminds were based in the Karl Liebknecht House, the communist murder headquarters. This is also where the murderers are said to have obtained "permission" to shoot Horst Wessel.

The elimination of Wessel was a done deal here long before the crime. Not only that, but after the crime they used the most poisonous arrows they could get their hands on. They insulted the dead man and tried to portray the assassination as a suicide attempt in order to deflect suspicion away from the Communist Party.

The main perpetrator and the murderer of Horst Wessel, a notorious criminal, was kept in hiding in Willen by higher communist functionaries immediately after the crime and deported across the border to Prague through the "Rote Hilfe."[8] When he ran out of money there, he returned to Germany. In Berlin he could then be arrested together with many other accomplices.

In court, these creatures admitted that they had committed the crime because Wessel had spoken against the state and against the Jews.

There were almost exclusively shady individuals with criminal records in the courtroom, all of whom were defended by Jewish lawyers.

When the verdict became known, which in its leniency almost incited new acts of homicide and struck German people as a mockery, countless fists were clenched in Germany.

The following were sentenced for joint manslaughter and unauthorized possession of weapons:

Ali Höhler and Rückert to six years and one month in prison, and

---

[8] The Red Aid: The German branch of the International Red Aid.

five years loss of privilege; Kandulski for joint manslaughter to five years and one month in prison, and five years loss of privilege; Frau Salm to one year and six months in prison; and Max Sambrowski to two years in prison. Joneck received one year in prison; Willi and Walter Sambrowski received one and a half years in prison. The accused Else Cohn received one year in prison and the assistants Kupferstein, Will, Sander, and Drewins received four months in prison.

We know that the answer to this murder will one day have to be entrusted to a German court.

In the center of Berlin, in the middle of the gray sea of buildings, lies the St. Nikolai cemetery like a piece of hope. This simple cemetery has already become a place of pilgrimage. Hundreds of German people come here every day to commemorate Horst Wessel, who has already become a myth, resting here under an evergreen mound adorned with flowers, next to his brother and his father. Unknown hands always lay flowers on the grave—people, men, women, and children always stand here and greet the one whose name and spirit have become immortal. Later generations will only become more conscious of the great sacrifice Horst Wessel made for the nation. In Horst Wessel we have lost a man whose great talent and innate sense of leadership gave the National Socialist freedom movement cause for the highest hopes. His death has left an unfilled gap in the front line of the leadership. Wherever he appeared, his effect was like a cleansing fire. Fortunate are those who were allowed to meet him in person; they will be able to preserve precious memories for the rest of their lives.

In a time of political and moral decay, a young German sacrificed himself here for his people and thus proved the greatness and sublimity of an idea that has since become the purpose of life for millions of people.

> *Bald flattern Hitlerfahnen über allen Straßen;*
> *die Knechtschaft dauert nur noch kurze Zeit.[9]*

Is this time not within our reach? It won't be long before our standards are waving over free German lands. One day, when

---

[9] "Soon Hitler flags will flutter over all streets; bondage lasts but a short time."

children in schools are told of the time of German humiliation and servitude and of the heroism of a young, waking nation fighting against it, they will not be able to avoid the name of Horst Wessel, who joined the ranks of the freedom fighters who paid for their love of Germany with their life.

Horst Wessel became the *Sturmführer* of all National Socialists who perished under the swastika banner for the ideals of Adolf Hitler. For us living, however, he is a role model and an incentive to complete what he and all the others gave their lives for.

Von Allen den Kameraden

Von allen den Kameraden war keiner so lieb und so gut
Wie unser Sturmführer Wessel, ein lustiges Hakenkreuzblut.

Wir saßen so fröhlich beisammen in einer stürmischen Nacht,
Mit seinen Freiheitsliedern hat er uns so mutig gemacht.

Da kam eine feindliche Kugel von roter Mordbubens hand.
Horst Wessel ließ sein Leben für Freiheit und Vaterland!

Berliner SA. -Kameraden, die gruben ihm ein Grab,
Und die ihn am liebsten hatten, die senkten den Toten hinab.

Schlaf wohl, du Sturmführer Wessel! Du tatest stets deine Pflicht.
Noch leben SA. -Kameraden, die halten dereinst dann Gericht. [10]

---

[10] The original song stems from 1915 and is about the death of a soldier named Karl Gustav Ulbach in France. It was originally called "Der kleine Trompeter" ("The Little Trumpeter") because Ulbach was responsible for relaying signals using a trumpet. In 1925, the Red Front changed the lyrics after a member, Fritz Weineck who played the horn in a band, died of a shot wound by the police. In the 1930s, the Horst Wessel variant was created in memory of his death.

Of All the Comrades

Of all the comrades, none was as kind and as good
As our *Sturmführer* Wessel, a jolly swastika blood.

We sat together so happily on a stormy night,
With his freedom songs he made us so brave.

Then came an enemy bullet from the hand of a red murderer.
Horst Wessel gave his life for freedom and fatherland!

Berlin SA-Comrades dug him a grave,
And those who loved him most, lowered the dead.

Sleep well, *Sturmführer* Wessel! You always did your duty.
There are still SA comrades alive, who will one day pass
    judgment.

SONGS BY HORST WESSEL

Wir Tragen an Unserm Braunen Kleid

Wir tragen an unserm braunen Kleid
Die Sturmnummer 5 am Kragen.
Und wenn es gilt, sind wir stets bereit,
Für Deutschland das Leben zu wagen.
Ja, wir sind Nationalsozialisten genannt,
Als 5. Sturmabteilung bekannt.

Ob Ausmarsch oder Versammlungsschlacht,
Wir müssen es immer beweisen.
Ob vor uns die Schupopistole kracht,
Ob die Luft voller Steine und Eisen,
Ja, in jedem Falle geht Mann für Mann
Vom 5. Sturm an den Feind heran.

Für uns da gibt es kein Hindernis,
Vor uns da muß alles weichen.
Wo wir angreifen, da ist es gewiß,
Daß die Unsern den Sieg erreichen.
Wo andere greifen vergeblich an,
Da zieht man den 5. Sturm heran.

We Wear on Our Brown Shirt

We wear on our brown shirt
The storm number 5 on our collar.
And when it's time, we're always ready,
To risk our lives for Germany.
Yes, we are called National Socialists,
Known as the 5th Sturmabteilung.

Whether marching out or fighting at rallies,
We must always prove ourselves.
Whether the Schupo pistol bangs in front of us,[11]
Whether the air is full of stones and iron,
Yes, in every case, man for man
From the 5th Storm towards the enemy.

For us there is no obstacle,
Before us all must give way.
Where we attack, there it is certain,
That ours will achieve victory.
Where others attack in vain,
There we bring in the 5th Storm.

---

[11] Schupo refers to Schutzpolizei.

Edelweißlied

So hell das Auge, so ehern die Stirn,
Wir tragen das Zeichen vom Gletscherfirn.
Wir treten an in Hitze und Eis,
Die Sturmabteilung vom Edelweiß
Im braunen Hitlerregiment.

Wir kämpfen gegen das rote Berlin.
Man hat uns verlacht, man hat uns bespien.
Mag kommen, was wolle, es kennt ja den Preis
Die Sturmabteilung vom Edelweiß
Im braunen Hitlerregiment.

Herr Vater, Frau Mutter, herztausiger Schatz,
Bei euch hat der fremde Brigant keinen Platz!
Ihn jaget zum Henker auf Hitlers Geheiß
Die Sturmabteilung vom Edelweiß
Im braunen Hitlerregiment.

Beim letzten Abschied im letzten Quartier,
Die schwarzbraunen Mädchen zergrämten sich schier.
Und dann sie küßten so innig, so heiß
Die Sturmabteilung vom Edelweiß
Im braunen Hitlerregiment.

Edelweiß Song

So bright the eye, so brazen the brow,
We bear the mark of the glacier's firn.
We face the heat and the cold,
The Sturmabteilung of the Edelweiß
In the brown Hitler regiment.

We fight against red Berlin.
We have been ridiculed, we have been mocked.
Come what may, it knows the price
The Sturmabteilung of the Edelweiß
In the brown Hitler regiment.

Mr. Father, Mrs. Mother, dear heart,
With you the foreign bandit has no place!
He will be hunted down at Hitler's command
The Sturmabteilung of the Edelweiß
In the brown Hitler regiment.

At the last farewell in the last minute,
The blunt girls almost burst into a frenzy.[12]
And then they kissed so tenderly, so ardently
The Sturmabteilung of the Edelweiß
In the brown Hitler regiment.

---

[12] *Schwarzbraunen* is translated as "blunt." The literal meaning is black-brown, but the figurative meaning given here is "straightforward, to the point, unfiltered."

Horst-Wessel-Lied

Die Fahne hoch! Die Reihen dicht geschlossen!
SA. marschiert mit ruhig festem Schritt.
Kameraden, die Rotfront und Reaktion erschossen,
Marschiern im Geist in unsern Reihen mit.

Die Straße frei den braunen Bataillonen!
Die Straße frei dem Sturmabteilungsmann!
Es schaun aufs Hakenkreuz voll Hoffnung schon Millionen.
Der Tag für Freiheit und für Brot bricht an.

Zum letztenmal wird nun Appell geblasen!
Zum Kampfe stehn wir alle schon bereit.
Bald flattern Hitlerfahnen über allen Straßen.
Die Knechtschaft dauert nur noch kurze Zeit!

Die Fahne hoch! Die Reihen dicht geschlossen!
SA. marschiert mit ruhig festem Schritt.
Kameraden, die Rotfront und Reaktion erschossen,
Marschiern im Geist in unsern Reihen mit.

Horst Wessel Song

Raise the flag! The ranks tightly closed!
The SA marches with calm, steady step.
Comrades shot by Red Front and reactionaries
March in spirit within our ranks.

Clear the streets for the brown battalions,
Clear the streets for the Sturmabteilung man!
Millions are looking upon the swastikas full of hope,
The day of freedom and of bread dawns!

For the last time, the call to arms resounds!
For the fight, we all stand prepared!
Already Hitler's banners fly over all the streets.
The time of bondage will last but a little while now!

Raise the flag! The ranks tightly closed!
The SA marches with calm, steady step.
Comrades shot by Red Front and reactionaries
March in spirit within our ranks.

REMEMBERING HORST WESSEL

The New *Sturmführer*

The East of Berlin had always been the domain of Marxism. One of the most important strongholds was the Friedrichshain district. Near it, is the Silesian railway station! Here is the arrival point of all Galicians, Polish, and all the individuals from the Far East. The Silesian railway station! That means desolate, ugly streets, taverns, subhumans, and pimps. Marxism is at home here; this is where it has nested.

Around this station stretches the district of Friedrichshain, a city in itself with its more than three hundred and forty thousand inhabitants. This grim neighborhood was to become Horst Wessel's battlefield.

In Troop 34 of Standard 5, everything went haywire. Discipline, fighting spirit, and comradeship increasingly faded away, and with them, above all, the members. An impossible state of affairs—a tiny, insignificant, internally divided squad was supposed to help the ideology of National Socialism break through in the deep red district of Friedrichshain?

This bunch was supposed to stand up to an army of bloodthirsty communist murder bandits? Twenty, thirty SA members against a hundred thousand? A grotesque undertaking!

The terror was outrageous. The enemy was aware of their superiority and exploited it brutally. We were powerless to oppose them. Nothing would have seemed more ridiculous than if someone had said at that time that we intended to break the terror!

The most outlandish characters usually try their hand as leaders with more good will than skill. We were a wreck, drifting without a rudder. It was a shame.

But one day the strangest rumors were buzzing around the squad and the section.

A new leader had arrived and was to take over the squad. The many disappointments had made people extremely suspicious. But there had to be something about this new leader. People talked about him all the time. His name was on everyone's lips, and everyone got excited as time went on. And so the storm evening meeting of the troop was approaching. The vigorous advertising had not been in vain. It had achieved its purpose. Almost all the party comrades that the Friedrichshain section had to offer had turned up in Heinrich's meeting rooms. Next to the youth sat the elderly; the worker sat next to the thinker. Secretly, everyone had the highest hopes for the new leader, whom they had heard so much about!

Then suddenly he was there—Horst Wessel!

He introduced himself to his comrades and gave a brilliant speech about the political state of affairs, to which he added his plans and aims.

Who could resist him standing in front of everyone, hands on hips, neck proud, eyes gleaming, as he put his great idealism into words?

The people sat captivated and were glued to his lips. He could not tell them enough! They sensed more and more how he was winning them over. He wrestled for the soul of each and every individual.

This was the leader that had been missing until now. They wanted to, they had to submit to him at once.

When he finally called on all men to fight in the front line of the German revolution, in the SA, almost everyone, old and young, joined. All those who had recently withdrawn in bitterness from active participation rejoined. The result of the evening was great and neither we nor Horst Wessel had anticipated it. We had immediately become a storm and received the Storm number 5 instead of a double digit number.

This first evening already gave us the certainty that a fundamental change was taking place, that we now had a real leader and that the right man was in the right place. Horst Wessel had taken his troops, with whom he would soon conquer Berlin, by storm. Here the phrase "I came, I saw, I conquered!" was appropriate.

He himself wrote in his diary that he had gathered wonderful human material. That first evening was decisive. It created a bond between leader and members that could never be torn apart.

The story of Storm 5 began!

The Storm Evening Meetings

Horst Wessel went to work with true ardor and devoted himself to his task with passionate commitment.

He knew only too well where to start. The structure of the storm evening meetings had to be fundamentally changed.

The storm evening meeting should be the spiritual breeding ground of the SA. Here the comrades should be made aware of what they are fighting for and what they have to sacrifice.

With great skill, Horst systematically turned the previously boring storm evening meetings into training and social evenings. He realized very correctly that the prerequisite for everything great is the cultivation of comradeship. It was wonderful to observe how Horst was able to captivate even those young men of whom it had long been assumed that they would not be able to subordinate themselves. It was splendid how the student knew how to deal with everyone. It was not condescension, but deeply experienced comradeship. It was significant that he found his most loyal comrades-in-arms in the ranks of the most humble workers.

The storm evening meetings evenings soon took on a different appearance. Every SA man was very eager to get to work. They presented an extraordinarily characteristic, a colorful picture, even on the outside. A national community in the truest sense of the word! The drayman who had just come from work, dressed in the most menacing attire, sat next to the clerk and academic. Old, well-served people formed a front with young faces. None of those who entered this circle for the first time could escape the spell that lingered over these evenings. Here a band of the most fanatical fighters slowly crystallized. The individual SA man looked forward to this one evening a week like a little child looks forward to Christmas. This was his holiday, when his heart beat faster. On this evening he was with those who thought the same as he did, who had the same passion, and who were just as miserable as he was. The storm evening meeting was his evening, it belonged to him, and nothing could stop him. On this evening he forgot the gray, awful, depressing hardship. Here he gathered new courage and drew strength for the continuing struggle. Here his lips opened. Here he sang Horst Wessel's defiant storm songs together with his comrades. If he did not have this glorious movement, what was left for him in the world?

Soon no one could do without the storm evening meetings, and long before they began, people would gather and wait for their *Sturmführer*. When "Horst," as he was generally known, would then enter the room, everyone would rush toward him and shower him with questions and new stories. The evening always began with a battle song, and then Horst Wessel gave a talk on the political state of affairs.

In a wonderfully simple way, often combined with a lot of humor, he made our will, struggle, and goal clear even to the simplest SA man. Despite all this, he, the heaven-defying idealist, possessed a cool, rational way of thinking and assessed political events with extraordinary accuracy. He knew that our movement did not need mercenaries, not mere soldiers, but political soldiers, and he was eager to train them.

Night after night he preached to his comrades the high song of the SA man. "The SA man is the driving force of the movement. He is a savvy warrior who fights tirelessly for the realization of National Socialist goals. For him, the struggle in the SA is not an end in itself, but solely a means to an end. The brown uniform represents the soldier of our time, who uses good and blood for the victory of the National Socialist worldview, because he is convinced of its correctness. The triumphant march of the National Socialists without the SA is unimaginable.

"The mercenary puts his strength at the service of material goals. He is not driven by any moral ideals; he only wants to take. Conversely, the SA soldier must constantly give, sacrifice, and bleed. The SA soldier is the modern type of the political soldier, the first servant of a gigantic national movement.

"The SA is a *Männerbund* of National Socialist apostles who consciously and without pathos carry the red swastika standard through the German lands, and without weapons nevertheless represent the most powerful and invincible army, whose course of victory cannot be hindered by any other power."

The comrades listened to his words with great reverence. They believed him completely. He could have asked anything of them. They would go through fire for their "Horst."

He did not approach his people in a schoolmaster-like manner, and yet he held everyone by the hand as if with invisible strings. It didn't take long before the storm was in such a flow that everyone reacted at a glance. Horst Wessel did everything himself at first. Organization, propaganda, finance, and so on—everything was up to him until the right people were in the right places.

If Horst Wessel had finished the broad political lines at the storm evening meetings, the most important thing came next: he stirred up the SA spirit. How masterfully he understood this; how he carried people away with his daring attitude. Even after the first storm evening meetings, Horst knew that he had put together a combat formation with which one would be able to dare to confront the Red Front.

He practiced singing with the greatest of fervor. Almost every evening a new song was rehearsed, and soon it was known that Storm 5 had the most and the best songs. Horst often sat down at the piano himself and taught his comrades the new songs, which soon made their way through every storm formation in Berlin and slowly became accessible to all the SA formations in the Reich.

Storm 5 had gone from being a harmless, ridiculed bunch to the fright of all the Marxist organizations in the East of Berlin overnight.

Nobody Wants Us

We had to realize all too soon that nobody wanted us. The bigger the storm became and the more people flocked to it, the more difficult the question of finding a venue became. Small rooms were of no use to us. We needed large halls for our storm evening meetings and we were thus dependent on the favor of the innkeepers. One landlord after the other who had made our acquaintance turned us down after a short time.

First of all, we were an uneducated, unpolished crowd that would drive away customers with our presence, and secondly, no innkeeper would take us in because of our beautiful blue eyes. Only a few thought of having us. Not because we didn't want to please the landlord, but because we simply didn't have anything. We met in all sorts of places in eastern Berlin, sometimes here, sometimes there, like a bunch of conspirators who had to shy away from the light of day. This was in 1929—that was still a time when it was no trivial thing to be a National Socialist. We were regarded as outcasts, ridiculed dreamers, and troublemakers. Above all, the bourgeoisie at that time still pointed fingers at us and thought they ought to lecture us. Often enough, Horst Wessel poured out all his scorn on this lazy society, which he hated more than Marxism.

As time went on, there was absolutely no place left for us to go to in the east of Berlin. We had to look for adequate venues in other districts. Finally we found a room in the Frankfurter Straße, and we stayed there until the closing. It was the restaurant "Zur Möwe," which is opposite the house number 62, where Horst Wessel fell victim to the murderous bullet.

The Shawm Band

It had always been Horst Wessel's most ardent wish to set up his own shawm band. This too was very characteristic of him. He wanted to provoke the opponent; wanted to beat him with his own weapons. At that time, it was almost a provocation if an SA formation was in possession of a shawm band. This right seemed to be claimed exclusively by the Red Front.

In those days, if a shawm band played its fascinating tunes in the streets, it could be assumed with certainty that a communist demonstration was on its way. There is no doubt that the music of a shawm band is both stirring and exciting. Another major advantage of a shawm band is that it is very useful for political associations. The instruments are relatively cheap to buy, and above all they are easy for amateurs to play.

Another circumstance may have contributed to the fact that the plan to establish a shawm band in Horst came to fruition. In the course of time, former communists who had played in local shawm bands for a long time also joined our storm. This, of course, made it possible for the existing band to train the rest of the members very quickly.

Out of all these considerations, the desire to be the first to found a shawm band in Berlin may have grown stronger and stronger in Horst, although it was actually prohibited from higher-up.

At one storm evening meeting, small sheets of paper were suddenly handed out, on which one could read the following: "Ten pfennigs for the foundation of an SA recreation center." At first it was hard to understand what this was supposed to mean. We had heard absolutely nothing about an SA recreation center; not even that one would be founded. We were faced with a riddle. So this SA recreation center must have had a special meaning. But we were soon to find out from Horst what was happening here. It had nothing whatsoever to do with an SA recreation center, but it did have something to do with a shawm band, as nonsensical as that may sound. Since the acquisition of a shawm band was not allowed, Horst felt unable to mention this in the donations sheet. After all, it was not a disadvantage to raise money for a recreation center. In the end, our comrades had more to spare for a charitable cause than for a shawm band.

Horst himself then told his comrades how best to distribute the slips of paper. He gave everyone a practical instruction manual. One should ask the next best acquaintance one meets if they could lend one ten pfennigs. If he fulfilled this wish, one should thank him very much and hand him the donation slip. This is how Horst explained it, and many comrades must have acted accordingly, because the money kept piling up. One day, what we had all previously laughed at in disbelief and considered a beautiful, yet unrealizable dream, came true. We were in possession of a real, brand new shawm band.

Although it was forbidden by higher authorities, Horst had prevailed. What all comrades had thought impossible, Horst Wessel's iron will made possible. He made a grandiose plan become reality.

There was a lot of excitement when the instruments were shown for the first time at the storm evening meeting. Everyone marveled at the gleaming things and was proud that they too had contributed to the success of the work through their fundraising efforts.

Horst was now convinced that they were practicing diligently. I still remember a parade, when we carried our instruments for the first time. The band was fully assembled, but most of the people had never held such instruments in their hands. We marched, the band at the front, through various villages and sang until our throats were dry. Everywhere people flocked in dense crowds and marched alongside the procession. The fact that the Nazis had instruments was completely new to them; they were seeing it for the first time. But why didn't they play? That's what some people might have thought at the time. As sorry as we were, we did not let ourselves be tempted to play, despite the pleading and curious looks of children and adults, because we simply could not. In the early days, it was pure propaganda to simply carry the band with you. This also aroused curiosity and irritated certain individuals.

Soon, however, the band had made such progress that it had three marching songs in stock, which it could perform more loudly than beautifully. At last we had reached the point where we could deploy our band. The other SA formations of Berlin were amazed and in awe. Everyone, everyone was proud of it and full of appreciation for Horst Wessel's achievement. Now we could challenge the enemy and show them: look, here we are! And how we lured the workers out of the barren proletarian barracks with our music. How often we saw disappointed faces. Some people couldn't understand it at all and thought the whole thing was a dream. How often we clenched our fists in impotent rage. But how many times were we greeted with joyful surprise!

Since the instruments were bought on credit, the necessary payment had to be made at certain times. Here again Horst found a brilliant solution that only he could come up with. Horst drove his storm as often as possible by truck on propaganda trips. The vehicles were then covered with banners, and most of the time we left the asphalt wasteland of Berlin on Saturdays. Here we marched through the villages with blaring music. Alongside the procession, particularly well-qualified SA members walked along, selling the donation slips to the inhabitants who rushed to the scene. The earnings from these rural propaganda tours were quite satisfactory, both ideally and materially. Through these trips, Horst took the comrades away from the corrosive, demoralizing big city for some time and brought them into contact with people who were living in a healthy and natural way and who were close to the land. The financial yield relieved us of restraining financial worries and gave us the opportunity to continue the struggle with undiminished strength.

We never had to worry about finances. Not because Jakob Goldschmidt financed us, but because we had a resourceful *Sturmführer* who always knew a new way out at the last moment when all else failed.

The shawm band soon achieved a certain notoriety. It was requested by people from all parts of the land and, in time, acquired a good technique.

A shawm band was still something of a rarity at that time, and for meetings and events it was a feature not to be underestimated. In the end, it also helped spread the fame of the storm more and more, giving it a better name.

Storm 5's authority was secured. The marching band was one of those features that made even outsiders realize that a genius was at work here.

The shawm band is solely the creation of Horst Wessel. Today it bears the name of its great leader with pride and reverence.

How to Break the Red Terror

Whoever gives us their hand, we will give it to them, but whoever shows us their fist, we will smash it open.

– Adolf Hitler

Terror has always been the weapon of Marxism, which knew how to wield it with astonishing virtuosity. The SA members of Storm 5 were exposed to this terror every day. At all times they were confronted with the bloodthirsty grimace of red sub-humanity. The red terror triumphed in the East of Berlin. It believed it could eternalize its reign of terror here. Any SA member of Storm 5 was in the front line of the movement and had to be aware that tomorrow he could be a victim of the Bolshevik beasts. Almost every storm evening meeting was an opportunity to learn how much blood had been shed in the past days. Here one could experience how the terror of the enemy welded people together and how unquenchable hatred grew in the hearts of the SA men. Horst taught his people to love their fellow Germans, to love everything that was German, but he also stirred up hatred against everything anti-German, against all enemies of our movement and against the degenerate sub-humanity that believed it could smother a freedom movement with brutal acts of murder.

He himself had tasted terror enough, but that had only made him more fanatical.

Many a beaten-up SA member was restored to health by the fearlessness and boldness of his *Sturmführer*. His words gave them new strength and pushed them forward again. Horst Wessel's SA comrades were shown the red terror after every evening meeting, when they had to escort some of their threatened comrades home. Then they could watch the figures in the dark streets playing the innocent passer-by, but in reality, they were waiting for the right opportunity when they could put a murder weapon into a young body.

Horst adopted Adolf Hitler's principle here: terror can only be broken with counter-terror. He was in no way prepared to let his people be beaten down without a fight, but went over to the defense right from the start. The longer Horst led the storm, the more brisk it became, and the more the comrades were committed to their leader. Soon the first actions were carried out, with which our storm and above all Horst Wessel gained the necessary respect of the Red Front. Soon after, the red tsars of the east of Berlin knew that their autocracy was finally over. Terror nests were dug up with appropriate ruthlessness. In the East, KPD bars were visited by only a few, but reliable, people, and the innkeeper and those present were forcefully made to understand their position. In the east, Horst Wessel soon made a breach, through which the brown tide now broke ceaselessly and conquered ground piece by piece. But it was not only in the east that Horst countered the Red Front, but also in other parts of Berlin. In the south-east of the city, communist terrorists played their vicious game and terrified the population. Not a day went by without National Socialists being beaten up in the streets. Attacks on the Wiener Garten pub were the order of the day. "Where others attack in vain, you call in Storm 5"—that seemed to have got around by now. So one day we were actually "called in" and were supposed to put an end to the nightmare. The evening meeting was over pretty quickly because of the event, and only the most necessary things were discussed. Horst gave general instructions about the planned action, called the *Unterführer* to him and gave them further instructions. Then it was time to carefully set the timers. In groups of two and three men, the storm moved to the south-east. A pub, which was to be regarded as the central point of the terrorist operations, was to be taken by surprise. The storm was divided into different squads which gathered at certain points. It was not a confidence-inspiring picture that presented itself to the onlooker. Vicious figures lurked about here in the darkness of the night. The whole thing almost gave the impression of a band of robbers. From the benches, behind trees and bushes, everywhere the people of the storm stood around and waited for the command. It was already quite late. From a nearby church the sound of the bells resounded several times, then, suddenly, a messenger appeared: get ready!

As if by some magical power, everything came to order in these huddled groups, and everyone moved silently in a single direction. Everyone gathered in a dark street. A quick order and we moved forward at full speed. We turned into a side street. From the other sides, too, our squads rushed in, and in no time we had penetrated the notorious pub. It was bursting with people, and more and more people were still coming in. The enemy tried to get to the telephone— in vain, for there had been colossal characters occupying the place for a long time before that. The landlord and the communists who were present turned pale with fright and could not utter a word. What was the meaning of this?

Then Horst Wessel jumped onto the billiard table, which had only just been in use, and gave his answer to the communist terror. His speech was a terrible indictment which he hurled at the communists.

"For years the communists have been terrorizing the respectable inhabitants of this area. We caution you not to attack National Socialist workers. If you do, we will make you taste the fists of the German workers. If there is one more attack, then God have mercy on you! An eye for an eye! A tooth for a tooth!"

None of the red "heroes" present even thought of fighting back. They let everything wash over them. Then the storm left the pub and entered the road in two columns. A hundred dauntless figures! The whole street was in an uproar. People stood at the illuminated windows and marveled. They had not thought it possible that the Nazis would dare to do such a thing. Not a single swear word or exclamation was heard, the mere presence of this troop instilled fear in them.

Silent as a threatening wave, the storm marched in unison through the dark streets of the red south-east—an indictment and a warning at the same time. The marching footsteps of Hitler's soldiers thundered across the pavement, and once again a roaring "Heil" rose up to the night sky before the end of the tour. Thus the red terror was broken here too by Horst Wessel, and in the time to come one no longer had to endure it.

The Orator

With fifty-six meetings in 1929, Horst Wessel was second only to the Berlin *Gauführer* Dr. Goebbels in the line of speakers in Berlin. He belonged to the top ranks of speakers and was a popular figure everywhere. Nearly every evening he stood in smoke-filled conference halls in Berlin and in the villages of Brandenburg and preached the new great gospel as an enthusiastic disciple of Adolf Hitler. His tremendous temperament combined with his persuasive power carried everyone away and led thousands of fellow Germans to join the camp of the German revolution. How he benefited from his great oratory gift as a *Sturmführer*, when he inspired his comrades with burning words. Whenever he had the time and opportunity, he sought out opposing meetings and presented himself for debate. For the speaker of the evening it was not easy and a damned ungrateful task to give the closing speech. On many storm evening meetings we set out to honor an opposition meeting with our visit. No exception was made. We took on whatever we could get our hands on, be it Marxist or bourgeois parties. Horst considered the bourgeois parties to be just as great a danger as the Marxist ones.

At one storm evening meeting we had learned by coincidence that the German majority party was holding a so-called meeting in the vicinity, in Heinrich's Festsälen.

We still had to smooth things over with the innkeeper, who had kicked us out onto the street like so many others. Incidentally, Horst wanted to give his people a little laugh and the people at the meeting a harmless scare. On the whole, these discussions were quite fruitful and served the SA members well. They got to know the opponents of all varieties, heard enough about their aims and were thus armed against all attacks. Since these discussions, thanks to Horst Wessel's skills, always ended in a terrible defeat for the opponent, the members were strengthened more and more in their conviction as time went on. A powerful sense of victory took hold in their hearts. These conflicts proved to the people again and again the superiority and correctness of the National Socialist worldview. This was a practical lesson that was more useful than dry, boring instructions. That evening, when the storm left in small groups and the first people without collars and ironed trousers entered the room, it was an amusing sight to see how the "revered" people present were quite indignant about the unwanted visitors. At first a few people came, then more and more, until the whole room was packed. Here the SA men saw the reaction in front of them. The eternally-strict who couldn't point fingers at them often enough. This bourgeois decadence usually avoided people like the ones who suddenly appeared here in everyday life. A picture like the one presented to the observer here was all too rare for a majority party meeting; it was more of a celebration of the status of the majority party. At first, there was a lot of shuffling of chairs. Umbrellas were fetched and the bravest of the "heroes" left the hall in a hurry with terrible goose bumps. Who should they be but communists who wanted to break up the meeting? If one only knew to which political orientation the people belonged, then one could at least orient oneself a little according to that and change one's ways if need be. Such thoughts must have been running through the mind of the speaker, who had just before hurled his words of wisdom into the assembly in a pathetic fashion and with great posing.

At first, the speaker's tongue got stuck in his throat. When he had slowly recovered, the words of power with which he had previously presented himself to the assembly as a militant changed in a very clever way into a polite, corny, meaningless gibberish. In front of the board table were the representatives of the Volkspartei, characteristic specimens of their kind. Shortly before, they had drifted off into a healthy slumber. But now they were quite awake, stuck their heads together and whispered cautiously. The speaker stopped somewhat suddenly, it seemed to us, in the middle of the speech. Several aunties clapped their scrawny hands, and the gentlemen present cleared their throats in embarrassment. There was a pause. Horst Wessel stepped forward and volunteered for the discussion. Again, a number of heads got together, clashed with each other, and contemplated what they should do. Suddenly a small fellow with a huge moustache stood up and announced in an agitated, hurried voice, "Due to the time, a discussion can no longer take place. The meeting is closed." Great excitement ensued. Horst Wessel stormed forward and demanded silence. Then he began to settle the accounts and tore the mask off the cowardly bourgeoisie's miserable face. Pale and shivering, the party representatives stood there and took it all in. They could not leave the hall because the SA men had blocked the exit. Three times the salute to the German workers' Führer Adolf Hitler echoed through the hall, and standing, the bourgeois had to listen to the spontaneously resounding song:

Die Fahne hoch, die Reihen dicht geschlossen,
SA marschiert mit mutig festem Schritt[13]

We had shown these spiritual creators of the class struggle that we had nothing in common with them. Here we saw the old collapsing, scarcely defended front of liberalism and the front of charging, uncompromising National Socialism. When the police, who had been alerted in the meantime, arrived, Horst Wessel and his storm had long since disappeared.

Another time Horst had chosen a meeting of the Deutsch-nationale Volkspartei in the magnificent halls at the Märchen-brunnen to cross intellectual blades with the speaker of the evening.

Here, too, we attracted unpleasant attention from the other people because of our outfit. After we had listened calmly to the speaker's chatter, Horst was granted freedom to speak. With one jump, he swung himself onto the stage. That alone was enough to outrage some of those present. Couldn't he just gracefully walk down the stairs like others? Then he stood there again, hands on hips, and picked apart the speech of the previous speaker. He showed the people the uselessness of their struggle in a one-class party which had proved by its activity that it was incapable of breaking the chains of slavery. For about half an hour he fought for more valuable forces for National Socialism and showed the way to freedom. A wild applause thanked him when he had finished, and impulsively the people left the hall with a defiant marching song on their lips, carrying away everything that still had marrow in its bones. The hall was empty when the last of us walked through the door. We had reached our goal. Now the meeting could continue.

---

[13] Raise the flag! The ranks tightly closed!
The SA marches with calm, steady step.

The SA Enters the Fischerkietz for the First Time

Old Berlin, a piece of romance, a treasure in the hustle and bustle of the soulless and restless big city. The foreigner hardly finds this piece of earth. It lies hidden like a gem between the raised stone blocks of the surrounding streets. The Fischerkietz, with its winding, narrow lanes and crooked, cozy old gabled houses, stretches directly along the Spree. During the day, this quarter has the most harmless appearance, and the strangers who come here enjoy it. But when night falls, the red death lurks in the dark alleys. In all the taverns that the painter Zille so glorified, the scum of this big city lingers.

The Fischerkietz has a special place in Berlin's political history. Communist propaganda fell on fertile ground here, for in the alleyways and streets, misery is the unchallenged ruler.

The Fischerkietz is highly contested ground. But the originally small Fischerzelle, as the party co-operative called itself here, led by the well-known friend of Horst Wessel, then-*Sturmführer* Fiedler, gained ground bit by bit, and today the dominance of Marxism has long since been broken. In the beginning, Horst Wessel also fought in this Fischer cell, until he took over Storm 5. Horst Wessel lived in the vicinity of the Fischerkietz. Close to his parents' apartment was the famous Jüdenhof, which can look back on a respectable age.

This was the usual meeting place of the storm. Often enough, it provoked the almost exclusively communist residents by its mere presence. Here, too, one could see that the enemy soon got used to this spectacle through constant repetition. Many a time Horst Wessel's voice resounded over the Jüdenhof: "Storm 5, get ready!" But often the storm also greeted the rumbling residents with a roaring "Heil Hitler!"

The battle for this *Kietz* cost a lot of blood. The enemy defended themselves with all the means at their disposal. Armed attacks on our members were a common occurrence.

When the battle was still undecided, Horst, who was monitoring the battle for the Fischerkietz with interest despite his own work, decided to strike a very big blow. As so often, we had made a propaganda trip and campaigned extensively for our movement. We started our journey home earlier than usual. We said we were going to drive through the Fischerkietz for the first time today. That was a daring thing to do at the time, and no united SA formation had ever done it before. The Fischerkietz was too chaotic. An unprecedented eagerness to fight was on the faces of all the SA men. A feverish impatience filled everyone. One could not be in Berlin soon enough. The wagon rumbled through the villages of the Mark, ever closer to the city. Soon the truck hurtled over the smooth asphalt, the flag bearer on the top, the fluttering flag in his fists. On the carriage they all stood, shoulder-to-shoulder, letting their storm songs and chants resound through the streets.

People appeared at the windows and in the streets and watched this brown Wild Hunt.[14] Now and then people greeted us. But mostly they shouted "Red Front!" at us. The city center came closer and closer, and soon we were there. Suddenly the truck stopped and Horst climbed onto the top. "No one jumps from the truck without orders. Everyone maintains absolute discipline. If we are attacked, then it is all for one and one for all!" Those were the quick words he addressed to his troops. "Get ready! Sing!" Slowly the vehicle rolled off—very slowly. "*Die Fahne Hoch!*" rose to the sky more vehemently and more ardently than ever. The truck drove around a corner. We were in the Fischerkietz. We sang, we shouted, and we roared. People were meant to hear us. We were there, unsolicited and unannounced. Everyone looked left and right, up and down. We had to be careful. The first faces appeared at the small, lower windows. Everyone thought the Red Front was coming, but what was that, the Nazis? Were they supposed to put up with this? This provocation— where are our own people? Get down on the street! The red mob gathered. Horst knelt on the roof, the shining flag above his head. We had arrived in front of the inn Zum Nußbaum, an old and traditional tavern. The whole area went into a frenzy. They came pouring in out of all the houses, the crowd grew bigger and bigger and shouted their "Red Front!" at us in a mad rage. They did not dare to do more. The determined faces of the SA men commanded their respect. Ready to jump, waist-belts in their hands, they looked at the raging masses. Then the truck stopped—what now? Horst stood on the roof and gave a speech to the residents. Everyone quieted down and listened intently.

---

[14] The Wild Hunt is a phenomenon recounted in European folklore in which an otherworldly group of hunters chase their spirit-prey. It is usually considered a bad omen.

"For years and years, the red terror has reigned here in the Fischerkietz. National Socialist residents are attacked here every day. We call out to you an energetic 'halt' and warn you for the last time."

When he finished, the street resembled a boiling witch's cauldron. Sinister individuals were gathering in increasing numbers. Unexpectedly, we had entered their domain. They could have crushed us. For the first time, the salute to our Führer and to the movement resounded here. The SA members were happy. Now they were in their element. How triumphant the songs sounded as the march slowly started. Curses were heard, which became louder and louder the further away we went. Through all the streets of Old Berlin we now passed, crossing the area until dusk. The red terror was broken without a drop of blood.

Crippled by the dashing, courageous performance, the enemy had found no opportunity for active resistance.

Once again it was Horst Wessel who, through this actions, took the fight for Berlin a big step forward.

Nuremberg

The Party Congress of 1929 came near. Everyone had been looking forward to it for a long time. Eager preparations were made in all regions of the Reich. This Party Congress was intended to show that our movement was on the rise, in contrast to the Jewish journals' talk of the decline of the National Socialists.

Despite the ever-increasing need, Horst was certain: everyone had to come along! He knew from the Party Congress in 1927 what a great experience such a day was. It provided new vigor for the future struggle and showed everyone how great the army of the newly awakened Germany was. Months before, Horst had already set up a "*Sturmsparkasse*" in which the comrades saved the money for the journey and for their uniforms.[15] So the day of departure approached.

On Friday, August 2nd, 1929, the storm gathered at the Jüdenhof with happy, smiling faces. The storm was almost complete. Heavily packed, it set off, singing snappy songs. The Anhalter railway station was bustling with life and activity. Finally we were on the train,

---

[15] Storm-savings.

pressed together like sardines. Now we were heading for indescribable celebrations. For some of the comrades, this was their first big trip in life.

The train rolled in. End stop: Nuremberg! Women and girls stood at the station and waved their scarves as long as the train could be seen. Everyone was singing! The same picture of joyful, excited people could be seen throughout the whole train. It took hours before silence fell. The excitement was great, the fatigue even greater. Soon everyone was asleep on the benches, on the floor, and in the luggage nets. There were quite a few who could not get a good night's rest and had every reason for it. They were quite audacious lads who originally had no intention of going to Nuremberg. But when they saw the excitement, they couldn't stand it at home and got on the train—and travelled to Nuremberg by station ticket. Around dawn, the train arrived in the hall of Nuremberg's main railway station. Everyone hurried, a terrible commotion everywhere. We rushed forward! There stood Adolf Hitler in the hall of the station. A thunderous "Heil" roared towards him. In the square in front of the station we were greeted by music and a crowd that numbered in the thousands. They saluted us. It seemed like a dream to all of us. What enthusiasm among the people when we entered Nuremberg. Who doesn't know the picture of Horst Wessel smiling as he marches into Nuremberg at the head of his storm? Nuremberg was spiritual compensation for the terror we had endured for years.

In the evening, it was time to line up for the torch-lit procession. The streets were jammed with people. Finally the procession started to move: a huge, endless line of fire. On either side was a cheering crowd. Finally, even the most stubborn of people was caught up in the excitement. We thought something like this no longer existed in Germany. We were only used to being knocked down, spat at, ridiculed, and persecuted. And now this? Our hearts were about to burst. We could have shouted out loud into the ears of our tormentors, "Look here, you cretins! Here comes Germany! An army of determined activists, growing larger by the day. The future is ours!"

We marched, staggering and drunk with joy, in the glowing torchlight, and the cheering grew ever more powerful. We passed the Führer in tight step. Music, singing, and cheering—it was too much all at once. One could no longer really categorize the many impressions. Then we went to our quarters. Every SA member held the slowly dying torch in his hands.

But what was that? A bus driver drove his vehicle recklessly into our column and wanted to get away. Torches flew through the air. Some comrades jumped on the bus, and the driver quickly learned that the Berlin SA, Storm 5, is a tough bunch to deal with.

Late at night we went to sleep. All of us could hardly grasp what we had experienced. Even in our most beautiful dreams we had never imagined it to be so great. In the middle of the night we were suddenly woken up. "Storm 5, get ready!" sounded Horst Wessel's voice. What was going on? Several comrades had been attacked by Marxists during the night on their way home and were terribly injured. During the day, the red hooligans did not dare to confront us. The night was their element. Here they could attack single comrades with superior force. Storm 5 had been ordered to clean up. Drowsy, we stormed off. The order was carried out!

The wake-up call started very early. When we arrived at Luitpoldhain, the whole area was already filled with sixty-thousand soldiers of the brown troops. It was impossible to miss—a tremendous sight. How proud and confident that made us. Here stood an invincible liberation army, Germany's last stand. Roaring shouts of victory, swelling into a hurricane, announced the arrival of the Führer. Then Hitler spoke to his SA. Then came the commemoration of the fallen and the consecration of the flag. The huge army began to move. The march of the SA began. The streets filled with people! The sun was shining. Indescribable rejoicing was everywhere! We were showered with flowers and confectionery. All of Nuremberg was in a frenzy of excitement. The girls came and handed refreshing drinks to the SA. When the march was over, people still couldn't believe that it was all real. Evening was approaching. It was time to say goodbye to the city that had given us so much joy and lifted us up from the gray desolation of everyday life.

Late in the evening we went home, towards the capital of the Reich, where new struggles, new terror, and new deeds awaited us.

We Celebrate the Constitution

Horst devoted all his attention to the opponents' tactics. He was informed about everything and was thus in a position to make use of viable and established methods for his storm. Following the example of the communists, he went about setting up assault squads. These assault squads were trained, reliable groups that were used for specific actions. Our assault squads were soon to find their area of activity as well. As a loyal citizen, Horst felt obliged to commemorate the celebration of the constitution, which takes place every year and in a dignified manner with great pomp, sausages, flags, balloons, and free beer. He wanted to celebrate the constitution, which today is being trampled on by its own founders, in his own way, but not quite as it was intended in the program. It was in his nature to always step out of line. He was happy to do without all the nice things that were available for free. He only wanted to give a nice party to the heroes of the *Bananenorder*, as he called the Reichsbanner people.

This organization, which protects the moneybags of the bank and stock exchange lords, which blocks the way to freedom, held Horst Wessel's complete contempt. Early in the morning of Constitution Day, the entire Storm 5 was already on the move. Everything was well-prepared. The dance could begin. In the north-east of the city we saw the first formations of the Reichsbanner. Suddenly, like a hurricane, the following rang out along the entire procession: "Down with the Reichsbanner! Down, down, down! Down with the Jewish defense force! Long live Germany! Long live Adolf Hitler! Heil Hitler!" boomed three times. The demonstrators were completely stunned, and paralyzed by shock. Then police jumped in and beat and arrested indiscriminately. But again and again, the chanters went into action, loudly expressing their contempt for the international servants of capital.

The storm had regrouped at the *Schloßbrücke*; many comrades were missing.[16] A fruit dealer was standing there. Everyone bought bananas. The man was doing a brilliant deal. Out of this, Storm 5 formed a line, presented the bright yellow bananas, and passed the raging Reichsbanner.

---

[16] Castle-bridge.

Flags were distributed—they cost nothing. Everyone took as many as they could get and used them in their own way. Again and again there were clashes between National Socialists, police and Reichsbanner people, because the former did not want to be deprived of the right to walk the streets. Shortly afterwards, we came together and assessed the situation. Several large flags were gathered, resulting in a big cheer afterwards!

Horst then told us what else had happened and drew lessons from what had been done right and wrong for the benefit of later actions.

We Push Our Way Through

Once again, we found ourselves rumbling on trucks from Berlin late one Saturday evening. Through the night we headed north. The destination was Bad Freienwalde, a sanatorium forty miles from Berlin. The whole of Berlin's *Gausturm* was on its way, and so it was again a matter of getting everyone together for Storm 5 to remain in the lead.[17] For Horst, these big marches were always just a yardstick. Using the other SA formations as a guide, he ascertained what progress his storm had made and what it still lacked. That his work was not surpassed, he could see again and again.

Truck after truck roared through the night. Weariness and the cold, fresh night air soon silenced the singing. Headlights flashed through dark avenues, along smooth country roads. The convoy of carriages rumbled through sleeping villages toward their destination. We reached our first destination in the middle of the night. We took up quarters in a small village. The farmers of the Brandenburg region fed us well, and early in the morning we were back on the road again. Off to Freienwalde! Again we drove across the countryside. Propaganda material was distributed to the farmers. The truck meandered along unkempt roads. There was a man standing there holding his fist out to us. In no time Horst was down and people wanted to follow him. "Stay on top!" was his command. The truck stopped and Horst hurried after the fellow, who quickly disappeared into a farmhouse. He had thus escaped with fright once more.

The farmers were amazed; many rejoiced. "That's the way to do

---

[17] A *Gausturm* was a large organizational unit of the SA.

it," one heard them say.

We continued singing. We arrived in Freienwalde. First we amassed out in the fields. Then the march through the town began. The huge band of brown soldiers started to move, and Horst, as always, was almost at the front of his storm. We sang and marched so much that it became a celebration and everyone's attention was drawn to us. The small town had certainly never experienced such an imposing mass-march. Therefore, Marxist ruffians tried to destroy the deep impression that the march made on the inhabitants. The communists stood in front of a pub, feeling strong, and they began to riot. Every storm passed by without paying any further attention, but not Horst with his storm. From afar he saw what was going on. In no time at all he stood face-to-face with the people and got into a heated exchange of words with them. Suddenly, they attacked him. In a flash, two or three groups jumped out of line and in no time at all the case was settled. A short whistle sounded, and instantly the groups were marching along in full discipline as if nothing had happened. Minor property damage and bruised faces gave the provocateurs the time and opportunity to think.

The march continued to the market square, where a large military concert was taking place. Dr. Goebbels spoke to the crowd and roused them. Then, when everything was over, police appeared, accompanied by the red heroes. They were looking for Horst Wessel and recognized him immediately because he had a band-aid over his eye. After a short negotiation, he had to go to the police station. In the meantime, all the other standards and storm formations had departed; only Storm 5 remained behind in serene tranquility, waiting for their leader. Finally, after a long time, he came back. "Get ready, march in step!" On we went.

After marching out in Freienwalde, the entire SA was transported to Eberswalde, an industrial town not far away. With tinkling music and snappy marching songs, the SA marched through this small town, which had a reputation for being Marxist. Marxism acted as the sole master of the town and protested in all the streets and squares. Once again a whole mob had gathered in front of a pub, and as our storm approached, they turned to violence. The SA members could no longer be held back. A wild brawl broke out. Then the police intervened. They were after the storm flag. But it was in loyal hands. Comrades jumped in and a fierce fight for the flag began. The protectors of the regime beat the hands and arms of the SA members with their rubber batons—all in vain. They were not going to take the flag. The battle was decided in our favor. The flag was saved. Schulz, the flag bearer, one of Horst Wessel's most loyal and reliable comrades, was arrested. Four, five, six men had to subdue him. We were brutally beaten. Everyone got a little something; even Horst had to take a souvenir with him.

It was difficult to restore order to the storm. With restrained anger, tight lips, and clenched fists, we marched on, inspired by only one thought: cheers to the next day!

In the evening, as the trucks brought us home and many of us sat contemplating, the defiant words came from the corner of the truck: "We'll get through this in spite of everything."

What Is Horst Wessel to Us?

When, on the occasion of the party congress in Braunschweig, the Führer Adolf Hitler presented the shining, consecrated swastika standard with the proud name "Horst Wessel" to the loyal hands of Berlin SA members, the thoughts of many SA men who had fought in a battle with Horst Wessel wandered far back in time.

How often had Horst Wessel spoken of wanting to increase his storm more and more until it had the strength of a standard? Did he ever think of a future development like the one that has now taken place? He must have sometimes dreamt of himself marching at the head of the standard he had built himself, his head proud, and his hand on his belt. Now the standard bears the name "Horst Wessel" in silver letters. Today, when it is carried through the former battlefield of the great deceased, his old storm, which is now already divided into three, and many other thousands of SA members, march behind it. In the streets the awakened citizens stand, take off their caps in reverence, and salute the national symbol.

An entire nation is awakening. Where previously the banner of Marxism fluttered, now the flag of German rebirth is flying high. Today, thousands of selfless people are completing the work of the dead *Sturmführer*. The spirit of Horst Wessel lives in every National Socialist. His idealistic, selfless work is a model for every German. Horst Wessel's martyrdom shows everyone the greatness of National

Socialism, for which hundreds of young Germans had already sacrificed their holy lives before.

Horst Wessel is the herald of a new era, the type of new German who, as a young man, placed himself in the political front because the old failed. The old no longer understood this generation, whose home became the political battlefield and the smoky assembly hall. This young Germany sacrificed its youth, its smiling youth, and like the young war volunteers of its time, became men overnight.

Scars adorn the bodies of the young fighters—their medals! The swastika banner rests in faithful hands. A new generation that knows how to live and die will reign in Germany and will keep Horst Wessel's memory sacred.

HORST WESSEL'S DEATH:
SHARED BY PETER ENGELMANN

The Report of a Nurse at the Horst Wessel Hospital

Between the narrow streets of the working-class neighborhoods in the north of Berlin there is a green area, in which lies a red building, once the Friedrichshain Hospital, today the Horst-Wessel-Hospital. The iron gate opens. Over gravel paths we walk to building number seven, a red, two-story house. Horst Wessel passed away here.

In the garden I meet Helene Richter, one of the nurses who cared for Horst Wessel for five weeks until his death. For eight years now, she has been caring for the sick and dying. But when the name Horst Wessel is mentioned, the memory of that sickbed comes back to life before her. She recounts:

Our hospital, which is supposed to be an asylum for all the sick and suffering, was the home of countless political victims, National Socialists and communists in the years 1920 to 1930. I myself did not understand anything about politics at that time; we only knew our work and cared for either the one or the other.

When I came to my ward on the morning of January 15th 1930, the nurse who had been on night watch told me, "Tonight we had an admission, a serious case. It's a political one, the professor had him put in a single room."

"He only spoke of his ideals!"

Then I stood by the bed in which lay a patient who could not speak, for his tongue was swollen thick; staples by which the bleeding had been stopped were still stuck in his mouth. The sign above the bed read: "Horst Wessel, 22 years old."

His temperature had dropped low, probably as a result of the heavy loss of blood.

This Horst Wessel now became one of my many patients, but it was not only his serious condition that made me particularly concerned about him; his brave demeanor, the whole being of this young, severely wounded man, impressed me again and again. In the first hours when he could not yet speak, he wrote his wishes on little pieces of paper. But soon the swelling of his tongue subsided, the staples could be removed, and Horst Wessel began to speak.

He almost never complained about his pain, which must often have been excruciating; he only spoke of his ideals. He remembered the details of the attempted murder exactly.

"I always thought," he said, "that one day I would be hit by one of these things. . . . My landlady must have been in cahoots with them. It all happened so quickly; I wasn't prepared at all. I was sitting at my desk, working, and I heard someone outside ask, 'Is Horst Wessel there?'

"I assumed they must be friends of mine, opened the door, and there, without saying a word, they fired.

"I still heard the bang, felt the blood running so warmly from my throat, but it all happened in a flash; they didn't say anything, but ran straight away; I must have fainted then. . . ."

Horst Wessel became very animated during such stories, and when he spoke of his goals, his big brown eyes shone. But he was happiest when his friends visited him, and they came every day. "I can rely on my boys," he often said with pride.

Once, when his comrades were leaving and were still shouting to him through the door, "Now get well, Horst," he turned to me, beaming: "Can't you be happy there, sister? That's why it's worth getting yourself shot!"

If he had understood how much love and loyalty his comrades had shown him—and I know he had felt it!—then his suffering must have been a great joy for him.

"We—we make history!"

Once I said to him, "Horst Wessel, I can understand you so well. My favorite poet is Fritz Reuter, who also served seven years in prison for his ideology."

"But Sister Helene! We and Fritz Reuter, there's no comparison at all. We—we make history!"

As lively as he was when he talked about his ideals, he almost always gave the impression of being seriously ill. He never complained about the severe pain caused by the bullet fragments still lodged in his flesh, only sometimes he told me that his throat hurt. That was the spot of his fatal injury. . . .

In the last few days before his death he became quite fresh and lively, as is often the case. On Monday I had the so-called pre-watch. Dr. Goebbels had been scheduled for a visit. Horst Wessel was lying quite lively in his bed and kept telling me, "Today my friend is coming! You have to leave him with me a little longer."

I replied, "Yes, but only if you promise me not to talk, but only to listen."

"I will, and what Dr. Goebbels tells me can certainly do me no harm."

Then at half past two, Dr. Goebbels came, and I told him that the patient must speak as little as possible. Whenever I came into the room, Horst Wessel asked me to let his friend stay for another ten minutes.

When the doctor finally left, he asked me as he said goodbye, "I have to leave for Munich; will I see him alive again?"

I could only answer evasively, but I found Horst Wessel lying in his bed, his whole face glowing!

"You wouldn't believe, Sister Helene, what a beautiful day this is for me. It's going so well!"

"What is *it?*" I asked.

"Our movement!"

That day he ate really well for the first time and assured me that it had never tasted so good to him. He was firmly convinced that he was now on the road to recovery.

The Last Hours

For a few days this state of mind lasted. But when I arrived for the second watch on Friday, the nurse told me, "Wessel is not well."

He never recovered after that.

Saturday afternoon I found him in agony already. The doctors were looking after him; he was given an awful lot of oxygen and injections. His mother and sister and his friend *Sturmführer* Fiedler were there. He asked me in the afternoon if he could fetch a few more comrades.

When he returned with fifteen of Horst Wessel's most loyal friends, he was lying in bed with his eyes closed, motionless, and breathing heavily. But as soon as he heard one of his comrades pass by, he raised his right arm to salute them with his last ounce of strength.

Mother and sister sat at the foot of the sickbed. I stood at his head; sometimes words still escaped his lips, but we could no longer understand anything. Friends kept watch outside the door. I stayed until one o'clock in the morning.

The following day, Horst Wessel passed away.

The Account of the Doctor in the Horst Wessel Hospital

This personal account by the nurse is followed by the shocking report by the director of the hospital, Professor Braun, who operated on Horst Wessel himself.

From his desk he takes a sheet of old paper, on the title page of which is written in large letters the name: Horst Wessel. It is the medical history, with a fever curve and some X-rays attached.

On January 14th, at 11:30 at night, it says here, "Horst Wessel was brought in in a severely bled-out condition. His face was covered with crusts of blood; he could not speak, and in order to prevent him from bleeding to death, immediate action had to be taken."

It was possible to tie off the artery, and the bleeding then stopped completely.

From the X-rays you can see the extent of the injury.

The bullet hole is above the corner of the mouth; the upper jaw is injured; you can see bone splinters and a bullet fragment in the cheek. The bullet has penetrated the tongue and got stuck in the neck in front of the second cervical vertebra, an extremely precarious area.

We fought the condition with the usual means, and the patient recovered quite well at first. But I still had the impression of a seriously ill person who bravely, almost stubbornly, rebelled against his pitiful situation.

On January 17th, Horst Wessel was able to speak again and consume liquid food; only his hearing from his left ear was still very weak. At the end of January, an improvement was noticeable, but we did not know whether the cervical vertebra had been injured by the projectile. Therefore I had the patient come over to me for an intervention. I tried to approach the bullet lodged in the neck with a probe. But I had to stop immediately, because the patient collapsed from the table as if lifeless. This was the first sign to me that the infection was progressing mercilessly. On February 11th, the condition was very serious. Fever attacks became more and more frequent.

On February 13th, there was an improvement in the general condition. Bullet particles and bone splinters were breaking through and we were already thinking *maybe we will make it after all*. But the pain in his cervical vertebra, which he complained of, was extremely worrying to me. If this bone was injured, the patient was lost beyond repair. Even the slightest crack in this vital part had to lead to a gradual decline, to blood poisoning.

From February 15th onwards, the condition worsened more and more; the strength diminished.

On February 19th, the condition was still bad. The patient was very restless, and the pain became more and more excruciating.

On February 20th, shivering appeared.

On February 21st, the patient became more yellowish and other symptoms of general blood poisoning appeared.

On February 22nd, despite all our efforts, it had become a certainty that the second cervical vertebra was injured and the patient could no longer be saved.

On the night of February 23rd, he quickly passed away.

In Life as in Death

We see a lot of pain and suffering here, and at that time we did not know who Horst Wessel was, did not suspect that this name would one day have a reputation all over the world. Nevertheless, even then his character was firmly imprinted on all of us. Despite his terrible suffering, his image was never miserable; you could see how he held himself together, how he rebelled against his fate.

We, who had to see so many deaths, will never be able to forget not only the hero, but also the suffering Horst Wessel.

PHOTOS

The parental home in the Jüdenstraße   *The Jüdenhof*

Horst Wessel and comrades at the Wikingbund

Horst Wessel at the Wikingbund

*From the Storm 1 days of the Berlin SA
Horst Wessel with the old guard*

At the Frontbann (1924–1925)

Trouble in the barricade quarters

Storm 5 in the East

On the sports field

Storm 5, with Horst Wessel to the right of the flag

Horst Wessel at the head of his Storm
Nuremberg 1929

SA marching

Horst Wessel in the company of his old comrades from Troop 34

Rest on the march out

*The house at Frankfurter Street No. 62, in which
Horst Wessel received the fatal shot*

The "Nußbaum" in the Fischerkietz

Berlin carries Horst Wessel to the grave

I had a comrade, a better one you won't find

Horst Wessel's grave

*"For everyone who as a pledge of freedom
Gives up his young life,
A hundred stand up in the whole country
And stand fast to the flag."*

– Heinrich Anacker

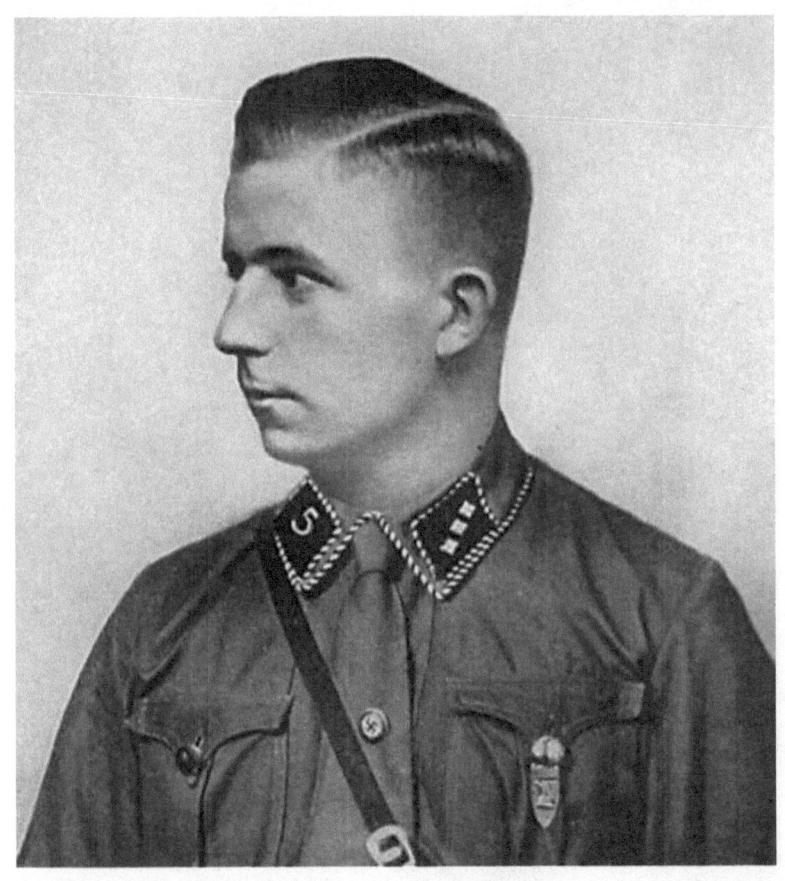

Horst Wessel † February 23rd, 1930
Sturmführer 5 in the Gausturm of Berlin

Standard Horst Wessel

SA *STURMFÜHRER* HORST WESSEL: A PORTRAIT OF A LIFE OF SACRIFICE

FRITZ DAUM

For Germany's youth

Painting by Karl Mühlmeister

THE YOUNG HORST WESSEL

Introduction

In the Berlin SA there was a *Sturmführer* who, with his clever, quick-witted mind, led his storm with skill and success against the strongholds of red communism. His storm troopers looked up to the German youngster with a confidence that could not be shaken by anything, and his fearlessness and unparalleled boldness carried them along into hard battles against overwhelming enemy forces. In his German heart burned that deep, pure love for the Fatherland and for the community members which alone enables heroic deeds. He was one of the most active and best fighters for the establishment of National Socialism in Berlin, which was the most powerful bulwark of united red Bolshevism and Marxism. He carried the swastika banner into the densest of enemy crowds and thus played an outstanding part in the victory of Adolf Hitler's *völkisch* idea in the city and the Reich. This blond, humble man in the brown shirt was the pioneer of a new Germany. His unshakeable belief in the mission and teachings of the spiritual leader, in whom he saw the savior of the Fatherland from impending hardship, was the driving force behind his actions and work. Keenly aware, he recognized that the red terror of the street, which held down the German people like a millstone and violently stifled every national movement, had to be fought and eliminated by counter-attack. No one else possessed the strategic dexterity to lead the SA's struggle in the streets as he did. With bold but calm daring, he and his storm troopers broke into those neighborhoods which until then had been the uncontested territory of the communists. The red flag with the hammer and sickle had to give way for the German swastika banner in his hand.

But the open struggle in the streets was not enough for his strong will; he visited the meetings of the communists and confronted them with the convincing force of his words, which came from a heart beating fiercely for fatherland and people. His words had a powerful recruiting effect, and through his eloquence, he drew countless people from the red camp into the army of the Brownshirts. And it was always the best and most active fighters who renounced the heresy after he had shown them the way. It gave him the greatest satisfaction that they became the most devoted, self-sacrificing SA men.

The brilliant successes of the young leader did not remain hidden from the opponents for long. No sooner had they recognized the immense damage this individual was doing to them when a surge of hatred arose in their ranks, which in blind vengeance ignited around the bright, strong, youthful figure. From that moment on, dangers surrounded his every move: a malicious, treacherous will to destroy his young life, which was filled with never-ending devotion. He knew this, but with an unprecedented boldness he continued unflinchingly on his way until his last breath, when tragic fate reached him.

Horst Wessel

It was the name of this National Socialist youth whose bright, young, heroic Baldur-figure strode through our dark days filled with the struggle for Germany's freedom. In his strong soul, the old Germanic heroic spirit had awakened anew.

His cradle was in the Weser region: ancient Germanic soil, sanctified by a historical past of more than two thousand years. Around the old oaks on the rocky ridges of the Weser Mountains, the mighty spirit of the battle-hardened warriors of Germanic antiquity still blows in the wind. They must have stood invisibly at the cradle of the young boy, bequeathing him their ancient fighting spirit as a gift.

When his parents soon moved to Mülheim upon the Ruhr, little Horst Wessel came to the Rhineland, which pulsated with a fresh will to live. Close to his new home, the green river flowed in its eternal bed, around which German longing and the love of an entire people had woven a shimmering crown of legends. As young as Horst Wessel was, given the clear receptivity of his Germanic sense, it is safe to assume that he received special impressions here in this historical land of battle, which has been hotly disputed from the times of the Romans and Germanic tribes until our own day.

Horst Wessel grew up in the safe haven of a German Protestant vicarage, guided by the loyal love of his parents. Here, in a family life filled with harmonious tranquility, the boy absorbed a strong German identity and a devoted love of his fatherland, and that which kindly shone through his childhood years: the feeling of belonging and solidarity with the German people, which grew and matured in the youngster into a strong, dominating urge of unconditional devotion, and which formed the impetus for his later deeds. And yet another foundation stone had sunk into the mind of the growing young man: the faith in God and the Redeemer. The deep religious feeling and the strong love for the country and the people formed the foundation stones on which the worldview of the young National Socialist Horst Wessel was built. Thus the powerful teachings of the great leader Adolf Hitler found the right, prosperous ground in the pastor's son and student.

Art also had a home in the house of the pastor Ludwig Wessel. It is easy to explain that this connection with artistic striving and creation could not have been without a determining influence on the gifted boy. It was the impetus for his later poetic and musical creative work.

Thus we see how Horst Wessel's parental home created all the preconditions that so strongly influenced the course of development of the youth that forces matured in the still-youthful man that enabled him to perform the deeds through which he earned himself an everlasting memorial in the minds of the German people.

Childhood days with their little sorrows and joys flowed away in the current of time. His father received the honorable call to work as a pastor and preacher at St. Nikolai's Church in Berlin. Thus the boy, with alert senses and a lively mind, came to the imperial capital of Germany. Here, at the center of intellectual and governmental activity, life pulsated more vigorously than outside in the country. The boy grew up in the imperial capital, and the big city with its diverse mix of people became his real home. Berlin was not only the city of diplomats and the seat of the highest administrative authorities, it also housed the first army corps of the German army, the *Garde*. Splendid military parades were a regular feature of city life in those days.

Horst Wessel's fiery spirit was also filled and enthused by this colorful, glittering soldierly life, as evidenced by the fact that he later belonged to various military associations. But it was not only the outward glamour of the colorful uniforms that had an effect on the boy; he also possessed no less an interest in the professional activities of the soldier. This was evidenced by the zeal and objective serious-ness with which he pursued his own soldierly training. Already at the youthful age of sixteen, he dedicated himself to training with a weapon. For him, this did not mean playfulness, but serious, pur-poseful activity. Soldierly virtues were highly characteristic of him. The idea of military service permeated his whole being at a time when in Germany the cries of peace from un-German leaders wanted to stifle any sense of defense of the Fatherland.

Horst Wessel's peaceful life, filled with the foaming, vigorous lust of youth, was blasted by the sound of the war bugles in 1914. With all the enthusiasm of a true German youth, his hot-tempered youthful soul experienced the triumphant march of the field-gray armies. How hard it must have weighed on him that his youth kept him from sharing in these mighty battles and banished him to the peaceful homeland, while out there, the guns thundered and storming armies hurried from victory to victory. But his lively mind craved activity, and like countless of his peers, he sought satisfaction in emulating war games. The quiet courtyards and squares near the Jüdenstraße, his parents' home, echoed with the hurrahs of storming crowds of boys, who played their war games with indomitable zeal. With all their might, the youthful hearts were urged to taste in a game the feelings of victory that their older brothers experienced in bloody earnest out in enemy territory. Horst Wessel's skill as a leader also stood out in the playful and childlike recreations. His inventiveness and his receptive spirit for all soldierly matters clearly qualified him for leadership, which was willingly handed over to him. Immediately after mobilization, Pastor Doctor Ludwig Wessel, Horst's father, had volunteered for service in the field. He knew that the soldier in the field needed spiritual encouragement and that he was closer to God than in the everyday peaceful life.

And the brave pastor proved himself in the field as a warrior of God, as evidenced by his invitation to General Field Marshal von Hindenburg's headquarters. Horst was directly connected with his father's tremendous struggle through his field letters, the contents of which poured into his boyish soul as it trembled before the violence of the great events.

One year followed the next, the mighty struggle of the nations became more and more bitter, and the warfare more and more spiteful. His pure boyish mind saw in the brave German soldier who withstood the mighty storms of the better-equipped opponents on all fronts, and in the brilliant leaders, the archetype of heroic devotion to people and fatherland.

And then came the devastating end, the collapse of the front. It was a terrible, torturous realization for Horst Wessel when he had to tell himself that nothing could avert this hard fate, that your people, your glorious Germany, had been defeated. From this moment on, a deep, contemplative seriousness became noticeable in the boy's character. He no longer spent his time at home, but in those fateful days spent every free hour outside when the armies, unbeaten yet defeated, marched back to their homeland.

What did he want in the streets, which he walked through in feverish restlessness? He wanted to look into the eyes of the returning soldiers, who for four years had fought like heroes and whose weapons had been knocked out of their hands by a stronger power, to see what was going on in their minds. He wanted to see whether the soldierly spirit in these field-gray men had also been killed under the force of the unfortunate armistice conditions of a victor bloated with hatred and vengefulness.

"Are you going away again, Horst?" his mother would often ask, full of anxious concern, when he put on his cap to leave.

"Yes, they say the soldiers are coming. I want to be there, Mother; you have to offer the good boys a welcome home, show them that you haven't forgotten them, thank them, respect them."

The sentences stutter their way across the boy's lips. His words reveal what is going on in his soul, weighed down by the hardship of the Fatherland. The mother's faithful spirit empathizes with him and clearly recognizes the painful turmoil in the boy's mind. With a loving movement she strokes his arm.

"So go, my boy, and greet the brave heroes for me, too," she says kindly.

Horst felt a hot surge of emotion when he found himself understood by his beloved mother, this true German woman. The plight of the German people burned painfully in the boy's chest. It gave him a comforting satisfaction to know that the same feelings were alive in his mother. A deep understanding wove strong threads between mother and son. And so it remained until death came between them.

He tirelessly roamed the streets of Berlin. Wherever returning convoys of field-gray soldiers entered the barracks, he was to be found there. His boyish eyes, sharpened by the deepest concern for Germany, searched the faces of those returning home, trying to read in their looks and expressions what feelings were stirring in their innermost being.

Breathing a sigh of relief, he realized that nothing of the shameful timidity of defeated troops who fled from the superior bravery of the enemy could be read in the looks and character of the soldiers returning from the field. Proud and undaunted as fighters, the field-gray soldiers marched home after the outrageously difficult battle had been concluded.

Horst saw many front-line fighters' faces harden when one or the other looked on with a disdainful look and an angry frown at the activities of the soldier councilors strutting along with red armbands. Young Wessel received the uplifting certainty that the returned undefeated fighters, who had to carry their weapons home under the pressure of a hard fate, were the true Germany and not those who, denying their German identity, spoke of a false freedom and international democratic fraternization.

In those hard and spiritually-pressured November days of 1918, Horst Wessel's faith in the future of his beloved German fatherland was strengthened by his faith in the frontline spirit of the field-gray soldiers, which he had gained from the unbroken courage of those who had returned home.

But it was in Berlin that the power of those un-German popular apostles, who in a false prophetic spirit pretended to want to establish a new free empire, showed itself most strongly. But nothing could shake or diminish the faith in the German future in the boy Horst Wessel. All these leaders and parties who presumed to reshape and master the destiny of the German people were, for him, only deluded phantoms, passing apparitions. He knew and firmly trusted that a day would dawn when the national flame of the profession of Germanism would flare up, whose scorching embers would destroy these alien heretics and their followers like chaff.

The distress that invaded the pastor's family from the outside was accompanied by the deep pain over the loss of the father. The doctors had recognized the pastor's suffering too late, and an operation performed at the last moment gave little hope. But before the suffering man entrusted himself to the hands of the surgeons, the pastor welcomed his eldest boy into the Christian community, pledging him to the care of the faithful God in whom he and his household believed with unchanging loyalty. This memorable moment was unforgettable in its shattering painfulness for Horst, when the father, leaning in the cushions, blessed him. A vow made under such emotionally moving circumstances also takes on a deeper meaning, and for Horst Wessel, his blessing had a lasting, guiding effect on his whole life. He held steadfastly to his faith in God's eternal guidance. It gave him support and confidence in a better German future, even in the most difficult of times.

Horst Wessel was a diligent pupil, eager to learn. He always considered it a natural duty to be hard-working. Horst Wessel suffered unspeakably in these hard times of need, when wild, agitated forces in the streets violently interfered with the lives of the citizens and the building of the new state. He saw how sources of pure and good nationhood were being buried, and desperately sought a foothold for his German sentiments, which were deeply wounded by the turmoil raging in the streets of Berlin.

He found the right consolation. The immense history of the German people is a yardstick of incorruptible truthfulness. What an infinite wealth of heroism and power it recounts to the descendants of a people united by blood and spirit from its earliest beginnings, from the time of Arminius the Cheruscan to the spiritual leader Adolf Hitler. As so often happened on the path of this people through the centuries, its splendor and power aroused feelings of envy and hatred among neighboring peoples. Again and again, sources of hatred burst forth, threatening to poison the German people, but God's eternal providence rules over it, and when the need burns highest and the collapse seems complete, he sends this mighty people a savior, born from its midst, called to a great task of liberation, who leads it back to the original sources of its true nationhood and prepares for it a brilliant ascent after an oppressive decline.

This is what the history of the German people teaches us all.

The maturing boy Horst Wessel also drew from it new confidence, new courage, new strength, and the foundation stone was laid for new faith in his people's calling.

Defending Oneself Is a Right and a Duty

In those times of transition from boy to maturing youth, the youthful spirit of Horst Wessel utterly rejected the way the ruling spirits and parties ran the state. They suppressed every impulse of national spirit, and for this reason they were regarded as enemies by the young man who loved his fatherland with ardent enthusiasm.

The fighting spirit that was alive in him demanded activity. His thirst for action demanded that he should join like-minded young people. So he joined the Bismarck League, but found it too narrow a field for the plans that lay dormant in him. Everything still moved in the ways of the old times, but he did not want to cultivate the old traditions alone, but rather to fight against the existing un-German order. He believed he had found the right thing in the Viking League. Here, the fighting spirit prevailed, openly rebelling against the political direction that put all that was national in the German people to shame. Horst Wessel was still a boy, but his quick-witted mind already allowed him to recognize the political connections in Germany, and the great love for people and country that pervaded his whole being sharpened his intellectual understanding.

With the untiring zeal that drove him in all things concerning his fatherland, he was active in the OC (Organization Consul). In this community the spirit of true defense lived. Tight soldierly organization and bold bravery were just what Horst Wessel needed. He had become a soldier from the top of his head to the bottom of his feet. Here again he showed his outstanding aptitude for leadership. In this young man there was a feverish urge to march in columns with like-minded people at a steady pace against everything that stood against and denied the German national spirit. The desire for a *putsch*, which lived in the bold crowd, surrounded him like the morning air.

It was the time of the election of the *Reichspräsident*. It was with great enthusiasm that the young Horst threw himself into the fray to campaign for the election of the aged Field Marshal von Hindenburg. Here he already proved his skill as a campaigner in the streets of his hometown, which were so familiar to him with their flowing traffic.

Horst Wessel's faith in the future and the militant development of the Viking League was bitterly shattered, and his flaring hopefulness destroyed, when Captain Erhardt, the leader of the *Völkisch* Youth, had to capitulate to the rulers of the so-called Weimar Coalition, which was made up of social democrats, democrats and centrists. The members of the fighting organization were stripped of their oaths, and the Viking League was dissolved.

The young people clung to their leader, who had prepared them for battle, with the faithful trust that only fiery German youths enthusiastic about high aims can muster. And now, shortly before the attack, which was awaited with burning eagerness, they were ordered to retreat. It was probably the most bitter and most painful realization for the hot-headed young man that he had to lose faith in the man whom he had not only revered as a leader, but in whom he also saw the ideal of a German nationalist, filled with a fighting spirit. Horst Wessel needed a long time to overcome this blow. He could not understand and comprehend that Captain Erhardt bowed to the opposing rulers and sacrificed his young troops, inspired by the desire to fight, to the compulsion of circumstances, while he had imbued them with a fighting spirit for the national movement and, if necessary, to die for it. Why not rather go down fighting and with honor than crawl cowardly to the cross? This was what painfully touched the soul of the young fighter: surrender without even having tried to fight.

But time and circumstances were far from ripe for sweeping away the prevailing un-German spirit.

Horst Wessel now stood alone again. His thoughts and aspirations were dominated only by the iron will to fight for his political ideal of a united national Germany, at any price!

An incident from this time is quite characteristic of the sixteen-year-old's combative spirit. For six weeks, no one in the house on the Jüdenstraße knew where Horst was. His mother thought he had gone on a hiking trip to some beautiful German region, knowing how much her boy loved his great wide fatherland. But where had he been? What had he been up to? The brave Horst had served in the Black *Reichswehr* as the most eager recruit and had gone through a strict six-week training course. He had become a soldier during this time. With the deep seriousness and iron will that governed his actions when it came to achieving his high patriotic goals, he marched in ranks, and practiced his handholds or his aiming skills with the rifle at the shooting range.

In particular, we are confronted here with an important soldierly characteristic that is a basis for all leadership: subordination to higher authority, which he voluntarily took upon himself by joining as a recruit; for it is the basic virtue of every dutiful soldier who is to become a leader himself one day.

Who does not think of the admonishing words that our all-honored *Reichspräsident*, the respected General Field Marshal von Hindenburg, addressed to the youth on the May 1st, Labor Day? "Whoever wants to command must learn to obey!" And that is what Horst Wessel did in earnest; instead of going on a summer hiking trip, he enlisted in the Black *Reichswehr* as a recruit! Thus Horst Wessel's destiny became ever-clearer: he had to become the fighter to which his spirit, his love of his fatherland, and his burning pain over the plight of his people inexorably urged him. But the sixteen-year-old did all this with a deep moral earnestness for a single high goal: to free his fatherland from un-German, gagging creatures, and to lead it towards a happier future.

He had learned to shoot; now it was his turn to learn fencing. He learned this manly art on the student fencing grounds. After passing his final examinations, he joined the Kösener Korps Normannia, and during his studies in Vienna he belonged to the Alemannia. Fencing was for his warrior-spirit; a thing in which he was fully involved. In doing so, he still had to overcome a great difficulty, because his right arm was weakened by repeated bone fractures. He couldn't quite pull off the blows; there was no force in them. *Well*, he thought, *let's try this thing left-handed.* But that didn't work at all, and so he mustered all his energy and forced it anyway. So he became one of the best fencers in the book, one of those who could book the most defeats for himself. He tasted the free life of a boy, but despite all his student-freedom, he did not neglect his studies, thanks to his deep-rooted sense of duty. In addition, hiking trips gave him knowledge of the beauties of the German countryside and established a connection with the people who lived there. Thus Horst Wessel's activities and existence, even in this time of free student life, were united in the one goal towards which his desire and will were striving.

Horst Finds the Way

The year 1926 finally brought the young man, who was searching for the way to liberate his people, the connection he had long sought in vain. Horst found the connection to National Socialism at a time when his spirit suffered greatly from the lack of a right area of activity and compassionate souls. He was lonely and sad after the failures and disappointments. It was not with enthusiastic hopefulness that he sought to join the National Socialist movement, for he did not yet know its real nature. What he had learned about it almost exclusively from distorting newspaper reports did not lead him to harbor great expectations: "Disappointment drove me to National Socialism!"

Adolf Hitler realized with his clear mind that he could only be victorious, that is, conquer the whole of Germany for National Socialism, if he fought the enemy at his headquarters and threw him out of his main position. The capital of the Reich, Berlin, was the seat of the rulers and the stronghold of false liberalism, democratism, socialism, and communism, which were alien to German nature. There he had to send his best and most capable combatant, for the hardest, most ruthless, and most difficult struggle would break out for this supremacy. So he sent Dr. Joseph Goebbels to red Berlin, where Red Front guards were protecting the rulers of the Weimar Coalition in the streets by outrageous terror and keeping them in their positions. Goebbels, the comrade with a heart full of fervent enthusiasm for the ideology of German National Socialism, whose fiery eloquence inflamed and carried away spirits, was the right man in the right place.

Horst Wessel went for the first time to a meeting where Goebbels, a Rhinelander, was speaking. The young man, tirelessly and almost desperately searching for a community related to him by blood, gazed at the swastika banner. It was certain that the burning red of the flag-cloth with the mysterious rune-like sign in a shining white circle excited him. He sensed a signal, a promise behind it.

And then this man spoke with the flaming soul of passion that felt and lived through all the hardship of the German people in devouring pain. First Horst Wessel was captivated, then enthralled. His young soul, purified and prepared by bitter disappointments and hard experiences, recognized the great compelling truth that here burst forth from German nature and communicated itself to the listeners, drawing them into allegiance.

Where hundreds of thousands of Germans had taken a long time in thoughtful deliberation to grasp the tremendous reason for Hitler's new doctrine of German National Socialism, it became immediately clear to the ingenious Horst Wessel that here beckoned salvation and liberation for his people. The hour had come when he could join the ranks of the fighters for a new Germany—at last! He, the nationalist with the fervent devotion to country and people, here became a socialist. Clearly and comprehensibly, he immediately recognized the essence of the new, German socialism, which does not only fight for one class and only seeks one-sided advantages for it at the expense of other sections of the people, but demands the same social rights for all community members.

And now, after he had familiarized himself with the essence of Hitler's German National Socialism, he saw in the red flag with the swastika the banner under which he had to fight for Germany's redemption from the unholy oppression of a lying international socialism alien to its essence.

How his youthful heart swelled as he attained the uplifting certainty that under the swastika sign there is a true national blood-bond, which he had sought with the hot desire of his German boyish soul. For Horst Wessel, Adolf Hitler's teachings were the German gospel of a new future for his beloved fatherland. But this liberating recognition of the truth of the great Führer's ideology was also connected with the irrefutable insight that no reshaping of individual parts could help here, but that a whole new Germany had to be built on the new territory of the National Socialist world view. All outdated concepts had to give way and be pushed aside in the face of the new classification in the *völkisch* way of thinking.

Thus the young Horst Wessel became a soldier and fighter for the Third Reich.

With astonishing clarity, his career developed with perseverance under the influence of his original German blood and spirit towards this one goal: to become a fighter for Germany's freedom against its enemies within. Against the false leaders who lied, cheated, and sucked the people dry, and against their Red Front, the mob of the street.

THE DEDICATED SA FIGHTER

In Red Berlin

The young SA man now wears the uniform of honor in the earthy brown color. The swastika armband shines on his arm; he marches along in the brown ranks. The brown outfit is the uniform of a German guard of honor and duty, which in Germany's darkest days took up the fight with unbroken courage under the enthusiastic impetus of a belief in a high ideal for Germany's future rooted in the German heart against a mighty superior force of malicious, vengeful enemies.

Adolf Hitler, whom German misery had called to be its Führer, realized that even with the greatest oratory and the strongest evidence, nothing could be done against the present rulers and their party comrades as long as the red terror of the streets, on which the opponents relied, was not broken. His outstanding organizational spirit also immediately invented the means of combat. He created the SA and for the first time established a political fighting force with a soldierly structure and training for the difficult struggle in the streets. Thus was born the brown army, which in this hard struggle prevailed and won against an overwhelming number of opponents, to whom even the most reprehensible means of combat were acceptable. From the side of the authorities, this brown fighting force was subjected to the harshest persecution, which sought to prevent its fighting activity with all legally permitted and unpermitted means. But it was not enough that the brute opponents fought them in a sometimes-inhuman way, and that the guardians of order of post-war Germany harassed them with the help of governmental means of power. A large part of the bourgeois newspapers, as the mouthpiece of the liberal bourgeois part of the people, showered the loyal fighters for a new, better Germany and its liberation with insults. In the press, these honest soldiers of the liberation of the people were called contemptible roughnecks and savage troublemakers. In blind ignorance and narrow-minded stubbornness, dirt and insults were hurled at those who fought, suffered, and bled for nothing other than to free this bourgeois section of the people from the oppression of intolerant red socialism.

But nothing was able to break the fighting spirit of the brown storm troopers or to paralyze their will to win.

Naturally, the SA's struggle was most difficult in Berlin, the red stronghold. The red waves of terror surged through whole districts, overflowing everything that opposed them. Here, in the most disreputable quarters of the city, depraved humanity stood in the service of the government forces from the red Marxist camp, ready to carry out the orders communicated from Moscow. This was a violation of the German spirit and blood that could not be imagined to be any harsher.

And there Adolf Hitler sent the eloquent Doctor Joseph Goebbels. But it would never have been possible for the great orator to hurl his flaming denunciations, his enthusiastic allusions to a new future for Germany through the lofty ideology of National Socialism, into the broad masses if the dutiful security of the SA had not ensured peace and order. The fighting hordes of the red organizations tried to break up the National Socialist meetings at all costs, in order to give the policemen, who had to obey the government authorities, the longed-for reason to break up the meeting and thus to silence the feared opponent.

Yes, one began to fear the bold speakers and their brown protection squadrons in the red camp, just as the frail and corrupt will always fear and hate truth and goodness.

Thus the SA in Berlin was engaged in an uphill, apparently hopeless struggle, when Horst Wessel put on the brown shirt and joined the ranks of the storm battalions of the Third Reich. This youthful soldier was filled with an honest man's rage, directed against all those who, in their blind party delusions, were making dirty deals with the noblest possessions of the German people. He declared war on them with all the strength of his athletic body and every emotion of his noble spirit. But he had contempt and the strongest condemnation for the bourgeois circles who, in their bourgeois irrationality and complete misjudgment of the real situation, cried foul over the struggle of the SA for the freedom and salvation of the German people, which certainly did not always take place in pretty ways, but which was highly necessary. There was no other way than to fight the battle with the means used by the enemy and on the battlefield that they had claimed.

During the following period of his life, up to the early, lamentable end of his life dedicated to the Fatherland, Horst Wessel remained connected to the SA right down to the last fiber of his thoughts and actions. The history of the SA in its bitter and relentless struggle against the red terror is inconceivable without Horst Wessel—and vice versa, Horst Wessel's life only received the consecrated glow of a German hero through his entry into the ranks of the brown fighters. The spirit that the great leader Adolf Hitler transmitted to this self-sacrificing band of pioneers of the new Germany was brought to its highest flowering by Horst Wessel's tireless, devoted activity as a simple SA man and later as a famous *Sturmführer*.

Just like the noble spirit of the great leader of the National Socialist movement, driven by the noblest will and the noblest love for the German people, spurred the masses on to new patriotic thinking in the time of deepest national decline, Horst Wessel's forward-pushing fighting spirit also had a stirring and inspiring effect on the comrades of the storm in his hometown, red Berlin, which was swept by the currents of political life.

But now the yearning soul of the young German had also found the connection he had long longed for in vain. These SA men, older laborers, tried and tested in life's trials, young students, young and old workers, and the unemployed, were all united by the same desire to live, or, if fate would have it, to die for the new future of their beloved people, as it had been foretold to them through words and writings by the great Führer. Their firm belief in Adolf Hitler's teachings and his calling kept them upright in the grueling struggle against a ferocious opposition ready for any atrocity.

And out of this unshakeable devotion to the idea of saving Germany and its reconstruction on the basis of a new worldview grew the most beautiful thing: the comradely union that Horst Wessel had sought in vain in all other organizations. Here he had it and it flourished in him.

The storm to which he belonged was a German community in which his work and thoughts were completely absorbed. How quickly he had grasped the value of the comradely evenings, which were supposed to bring the people of this storm, thrown together from the most diverse strata of the population, closer together internally. While the class mentality was being preached outside in the whole of Germany, and the party opposition was being carried out in an inciting manner, and the gap between the social classes and the people was becoming ever more profound, in these comradely evenings the German-blooded brotherhood blossomed between the men and youths who, in their tough battles on the streets, threw themselves with unparalleled courage and unheard-of daring against the violent red masses. The common struggle and the comradeship that broke down all barriers of class welded these brown soldiers together into a united force of tremendous strength.

Until now, he had not come into intimate contact with the lowest classes of people. Here he got to know them, the simple people working in carpentry and the baker's shop, the rubbish collector and the shipper. He knew how to welcome everyone, even the roughest of fellows, because in him the German blood and the belief in the spirit of the true national community were alive. How could it be otherwise?

After all, he was a Berlin boy, and as a lively kid he had romped through the open squares and dark alleys of Berlin around the Jüdenhof, so how could he not find the right tone to communicate with these simple graybeards and young hotspurs from the fourth, the workers' class, who were all inspired by the teachings of the great Führer and believed in him with the loyalty of honest people? Never, it is said of him, did Horst Wessel, the student, become preachy. In a simple, calm manner, he knew how to awaken the intellectual interests of his comrades in an effort to expand their intellectual circle. He had recognized the wisdom of the principle that only the spirit ennobles the purpose of every deed for which it is committed.

How he benefited from his poetic and musical talents! What moved his interest and spurred him on to national work emanated from his songs, and the momentum of his songs enlivened the storm troopers of the brown SA army in Berlin and far and wide throughout the Reich. Soon after he had first settled in, he became the center of the intellectual life of the Berlin SA. But it was not only on the comradely evenings that his aptitude for leadership became apparent; it also shone out in a brilliant, convincing manner in the perilous duty on the streets. Horst Wessel had all the good soldierly virtues inborn, as it were, and his brilliant mind made him a skilful leader. His fearlessness and calm audacity not only created a heroic reputation for him, but also moved the storm troopers under his command to extraordinary deeds.

But let us see what Berlin looked like at the time Horst Wessel joined the ranks of the brown fighters.

Hard Work

The intrusion of the National Socialist movement into Berlin was naturally regarded by the opponents as a bold provocation. They regarded the Reich capital as their very own indisputable territory, in the streets of which the red mob of communism had the sole right of marching to exercise terror.

But Hitler had decided to break the terror of violence by terror, and so the SA marched into the streets as ordered, to fight for the national cause there too, as in the assembly halls.

It became a bitter, difficult struggle. How small and scattered the group was at first! But no one retreated; everyone did his duty with a full sense of responsibility.

There had been a meeting somewhere, and Dr. Goebbels had denounced with fluent eloquence and unflinching vehemence the shameful economy of those in power. Only by summoning all their strength had the good SA been able to maintain order and forcibly remove the disturbers of the peace. Full of courage, the few had withstood the hail of rocks of a jeering, angry crowd. The small group had boldly counterattacked against the wild crowd of Red Front fighters in order to shield the doctor from the attacks of the raging mob.

When they got him safely into the car, the windows of which were still being smashed by rocks as they drove away, they went home in a closed group. The scum of Wedding in Berlin already knew the strength of the brown SA. As long as they were together, they held back cowardly. But eventually, one or two of them had to pass through a dark alley or a gloomy corner. They crept home through the night with close attention. Suddenly, however, three or four or more savage fellows with clubs or iron bars burst out of a hiding place. Blows rained down on the defenseless men, who lay bleeding and grunting on the ground, while the cowardly gang hurriedly made their way to safety after the deed was done. It gave these dehumanized fellows great pleasure to have once again put one of the hated brown men out of action. They had nothing that seemed holy and worthy of veneration, neither German blood ties nor faith in God, but only bare, blatant greed, the desire for pleasure, and hatred for all those who had saved something through honest work. None of these red murdering bandits knew anything of the sacred concept of fatherland and the community member; the red leaders had made that contemptible to them and dragged it down through ridicule.

It also happened that several SA men walked together through a busy street in a feeling of certain security, until suddenly one of them collapsed screaming, hit by the murdering steel of a treacherous coward who ducked into the crowd shielding him.

The history of the Berlin SA is full of such and similar murders.

The red organizations had believed that they could destroy the weak storm troopers right at the beginning. After a short time, however, they had to realize that they were hitting a brick wall. Their rage increased to the point of mad fury, and the struggle became ever more spiteful and bitter. The Reichsbanner and Red Front united here to repel the Nazis, for they soon realized that they had not only the SA of the street to fear, but that Adolf Hitler's clear, truthful teaching of German rebirth was beginning to draw many comrades of the Red Front over to the front beneath the swastika.

The rulers, too, realized that the doctrine of National Socialism was detracting from their own doctrine of international socialism, and that the call for blood ties and the unification of all classes was above their class-hatred and was finding only too-willing ears within their own ranks. Thus the police were mobilized and the law was applied with unjust severity against National Socialism.

Each of the SA men knew the inside of the police headquarters on Alexanderplatz. They had often been arrested, interrogated, and released. They laughed about it, and the officers soon knew their way around them; they knew that neither rough handling nor plain friendliness would lure any statements out of them other than those that the Brownshirts considered favorable.

Under the ruling system of the Weimar Coalition, the authorities and police organizations had been given the slogan of suppressing National Socialism and its supporters at all costs. The effect of this was that Hitler's soldiers were monitored and dealt with in the harshest manner by the obedient police authorities, while their opponents from the red camp were hardly noticed and rarely arrested. Thus, in a certain sense, the brown fighters of the SA were outlaws. Their opponents, of course, took advantage of this situation and, unchallenged by the police, allowed themselves the most outrageous attacks.

This was the situation when Horst Wessel, whose dedication and leadership ability had long been recognized by the authorities, became leader himself. His fearlessness and calm boldness, combined with his quick perception and precise knowledge of the attitudes of his red opponents, made him the outstanding leader he proved to be in the struggle that was now breaking out and growing more and more bitter.

The *Gauleiter*, Dr. Goebbels, immediately suspected the forces that the strong, radiant spirit of this upright blond-haired student could awaken in the movement and make it serviceable to the good cause. This conviction forced itself upon him even more when he saw and heard him perform as a speaker. Horst Wessel's talent as an orator had broken through overnight, so to speak. He stood up to his opponents in the battle of words just as boldly, calmly, and confidently as he did in the street fights. How could it be otherwise? After all, his soul was completely filled with the driving love for the people and the Fatherland, his bright mind recognized the plight of the people, and he saw clearly how the German people were falling deeper and deeper into misery under the brutal, selfish, and dishonest leadership of the greedy clique. On the other hand, he recognized in Hitler's teachings and in the new worldview of National Socialism the only way to salvation. The right words came to him, and he knew how to speak them with the convincing force of truth.

He had met the great leader at the party congress in Nuremberg. The irresistible driving force emanating from the strong spirit of Adolf Hitler also swept Horst Wessel away, and the power of his personality convinced him, too. He was shaken to the depths of his strong soul, carried by love for the people and noble enthusiasm by the impressions he received.

Storm 5

Horst Wessel's outstanding qualities were held in such high regard that when he was appointed squad leader, the district leadership allowed him to choose his squad.

It is characteristic of the young leader's work ethic that he chose the worst squad in the most disreputable area: Troop 34 of Friedrichshain.

He knew why he did it. This squad, consisting of only a baker's dozen of unruly rough guys, was rotten. It was just vegetating in one of the worst communist quarters and could only keep itself alive with great difficulty under the most savage terror of its rude, violent surroundings. There was no sign of any lively activity or even of any victorious advance and growth.

His comrades did not immediately understand the deeper reason for this choice. They reproached him for choosing this "worst pile of pigs," as they called the troop in their straight Berlin way of speaking, when he could even have his old Storm 2 or even Storm 17 from Standard 4, the famous Zackig Standard. No, of all places, he had to go to that desolate region that had the reputation of being a red stronghold. They warned him: "Stay away from there, boy! The red bandits have already pledged to kill you, you'll be in for a surprise in that rotten area!"

But Horst Wessel was not fooled. He calmly replied, "Leave it, comrades, it will soon be different there!"

And it did change. The change brought about by the spiritual and militant drive of this blond-headed leader was surprising and powerful.

Horst Wessel had listened to the words of the great Führer, absorbed them, and was about to put them into practice. He knew what Adolf Hitler wanted the SA to be and what high tasks were assigned to it. Not a secret political association, not a military association that cherished the old soldierly spirit and wallowed in old traditions, but an active fighting force with tight soldierly training and the strictest discipline. Their battlefield was the street, their enemy the Red Front of the Marxist government, and their goal was a new, better Germany.

And so Horst Wessel set about transforming the lost squad, Troop

34, into a strong storm troop of the brown SA.

For the first time he stepped among them and spoke to them. In addition to the thirteen, a crowd of curious people had gathered to hear what this young student, to whom the district leadership had incomprehensibly entrusted the leadership of the neglected squad in the most dangerous area of red Berlin, would tell them.

Horst Wessel let his eyes glide over those gathered and recognized sharply what kind of mindset lived behind the square foreheads. He saw from the often casually mocking expressions how little trust was placed in him here. But it was precisely this obvious resistance that appealed to him; his strength grew from it, and his unshakable belief in victory gave his speech its convincing force.

He spoke to them. Calmly and firmly, his mouth formed the sentences. In a clear form he conveyed to these resistance fighters the doctrine of National Socialism and how the ways of the great leader must lead to the unification of the whole people and to the salvation of Germany.

His strong spirit had been stimulated by the speeches of Goebbels and by the powerful ideas of the great Führer, so that something of the compelling power of these outstanding men was alive in him and burst forth from him.

He concluded by urging those present to take an active part in the great struggle for Germany's liberation from un-German leadership and red terror. It was not enough to sympathize with the movement, but to fight in the ranks of the SA for Germany and its better future.

When one of the fellows said in an annoying tone that they were from the troop and that there was no point in talking any further, Horst Wessel snapped at the speaker harshly and sharply, "If you are from the squad, then stand up as soon as you speak to me, your leader. I demand that you behave decently and soldierly, understood? Come on, get up, whoever is from the squad!"

Lo and behold—under his compelling gaze they all stood up. The squad was thirty strong after that first evening: a fine success. The oldest of them was sixty-five years old, and the youngest, fifteen.

Horst Wessel created a strong soldierly troop out of this variously-composed group through real training efforts. It really was not easy. It was hard to instill discipline in them, since they included people who had been through four years of war at the front and had served in all kinds of *Freikorps*. But Horst Wessel was adamant about strict order, and didn't let them get away with anything. The fact that he was nevertheless able to pull these unruly elements together into a cohesive squad was due not only to his energetic command on the training grounds, but also largely to his tireless care off-duty and, above all, to his comradely spirit. With a sure eye, he took charge of the spiritual care during the storm evening meetings he introduced. He devoted all his free time to the people, knew all their needs, helped where he could, and showed them that he was their comrade in life and death, whom they could trust in all situations, on- and off-duty. Thus the bond of trust closed around this group, which only weeks ago was held in low esteem, and it became the best and most outstanding fighting force of the Berlin SA, only through the all-pervading spirit of Horst Wessel, the young student from the Jüdenstraße.

The time came when his name alone attracted attention. The squad that Horst Wessel had taken over at the strength of a baker's dozen soon numbered a hundred men. But the most remarkable thing about the increase was that the best, most solid members from the Red Front switched over to him. This was only natural and easily explained. The thinking members of the red cliques had long since become suspicious, because everything in the Reich was going down the drain, and when they heard the message of salvation from the mouth of Horst Wessel, they were drawn into his ranks with irresistible force.

This unprecedented success of Horst Wessel's leadership naturally did not go unnoticed by the *OSAF-Ost*,[18] the supreme SA leader of Berlin. He felt it his duty to give the Führer, as well as the loyal people, honorable satisfaction. So he made the squad into a storm and, in recognition of their special achievements, gave them a lower number: Storm 5.

In this way, the spirit of a young German man who was passionate about the Fatherland and enthusiastic about National Socialist teachings spread further and further in the Berlin SA. His merits grew ever greater; his heroic reputation grew ever more firmly around his name. He was now ready for action.

For Horst Wessel, his devoted work for the establishment and consolidation of the storm troopers had another, deeper meaning.

---

[18] The *Oberster Sturmabteilung-Führer-Ost*, or Supreme SA Leader of the East.

Through his tireless caring activities in the spirit of comradeship, even outside of duty hours, he had come much closer to the people of the fourth estate than had previously been the case.[19] He had gained a deeper insight into their existence and lived their lives in often extremely meager conditions, feeling their hardships and worries as his own.

It is understandable that this experience could not remain without a lasting effect on such a strongly sensitive person as Horst Wessel. He, the pastor's son, who had never known physical and financial hardship, whose life had been secure, now saw how poor people had to struggle with the hardships of an existence made more difficult by their lack of resources, and yet how they fundamentally accepted the struggle for daily bread and all the other necessities of life as a fact that could not be avoided, often with a kind of grim humor.

The insights into the struggles of his comrades, whose trust he had won after winning their approval, shook him.

He, who knew Adolf Hitler's fundamental ideas for the reconstruction of the Reich and the people, and who was imbued with his teachings like few others, saw here with deep emotion how justified the transformation was in the construction and unification of the classes in the people.

Nothing of the economic struggle of the poor had ever penetrated into the secure equilibrium of his days as a member of a family of the privileged classes, and now he was confronted with the naked struggle for survival.

To help, to help: that was the first impulse that made him sacrifice everything he possessed. It is written in the hearts of his comrades with words of eternal gratitude, which he gave to them in silence and in deepest solidarity.

But from this experience of hardship he drew new strength and new motivation for his great task of leading National Socialism to victory in the struggle. He saw in this not only the salvation of his beloved Germany, but also the uplifting of the lowest layers of the population from a state of life afflicted by hardships of all kinds.

The decline of Germany under the leadership and influence of the ruling powers, which caused the lowest and middle classes to suffer

---

[19] By "fourth estate" the author means the working-class people. This is different from the third estate of the French Revolution era, which included these workers as well as the bourgeois class. Wessel is working mainly with the lower classes.

the most, clearly showed him that class antagonism must lead to the downfall of the German people. But he was just as certain that National Socialism, with its bridging of the social classes and the unity of the people into a community of shared destiny, was the salvation from the perilous situation. He saw how, in the state of class struggle for the proletariat at that time, the fourth class was becoming ever poorer and ever more impoverished, how individuals were enriching themselves through ruthless selfishness at the expense of the general public, and he recognized the hypocrisy and the false hollowness of Marxist doctrine. And so he threw himself into the struggle with renewed enthusiasm the more he became aware of the plight of the poor, for whom he was fighting, suffering, and arguing.

Horst Wessel the Poet

If we look at Horst Wessel's life and follow his inner development, it is not surprising that the German youth with the gift of the pen and words became a poet. A young person who experiences all the burning questions of his people and country with such depth of feeling will inevitably give in to the urge to put the experience that shakes him into poetic words. And Horst Wessel possessed the gift of poetry. It expressed itself quite naturally in the fight of the SA for Germany, in which his entire mental and vital energy was spent.

When he was appointed *Sturmführer* of the new Storm 5, a deep joy over the success and recognition of his work surged through his mind. He had to give poetic expression to this feeling, and so his "Song of the 5th Storm" came into being:

Wir Tragen an Unserm Braunen Kleid

Wir tragen an unserm braunen Kleid
Die Sturmnummer 5 am Kragen,
Und wenn es gilt, sind wir stets bereit,
Für Deutschland das Leben zu wagen.
Ja, wir sind Nationalsozialisten genannt,
Als fünfte Sturmabteilung bekannt.

Ob Ausmarsch oder Versammlungsschlacht,
Wir müssen es immer beweisen,
Ob vor uns die Schupopistole kracht,
Ob die Luft voller Steine und Eisen,
Ja in jedem Falle geht Mann für Mann
Vom fünften Sturm an den Feind heran.

Für uns da gibt es kein Hindernis,
Vor uns da muß alles weichen.
Wo wir angreifen, da ist es gewiß,
Daß die Unsern den Sieg erreichen.
Wo andere greifen vergeblich an,
Da zieht man den fünften Sturm heran.

We Wear on Our Brown Shirt

We wear on our brown shirt
The storm number 5 on our collar.
And when it's time, we're always ready,
To risk our lives for Germany.
Yes, we are called National Socialists,
Known as the 5th Sturmabteilung.

Whether marching out or fighting at rallies,
We must always prove ourselves.
Whether the *Schupo* pistol bangs in front of us,
Whether the air is full of stones and iron,
Yes, in every case, man for man
From the 5th Storm towards the enemy.

For us there is no obstacle,
Before us all must give way.
Where we attack, there it is certain,
That ours will achieve victory.
Where others attack in vain,
There we bring in the 5th Storm.

How strongly and clearly expressed in these few lines are the combative nature that urged him forward and the spirit of devotion! One can feel the lust and pride in the words with which his Storm 5 rushes into battle.

Horst Wessel possessed a great gift for expressing in words that which filled his soul, which belonged to the SA to the very last thought, and was completely filled with the urge to fight for the new Reich. Through their clarity and power of words, his songs also carried away his fellow fighters. They were first sung in his storm and taken over by the others, and soon resounded with their compelling rhythm wherever the brown battalions marched to fight against the red oppressive rule.

Horst Wessel gave his comrades and the German people a whole series of songs, chants, and plays. They are all imbued with the noble spirit of devotion to the cause of freedom, National Socialism, and the struggle for people and fatherland.

The fact that he often composed songs or texts for speeches in prison, before or after the usual interrogations, testifies to the extent to which he was imbued in all situations and at all times with his vocation as a fighter for Germany's liberation, and how completely absorbed he was in his devotion to it. Doesn't it seem like a symbolic meaning that the songs of struggle and liberation from the tyranny of the red terror flowed out of the barred rooms of the dungeon and inspired people for the new Germany?

The Winds of War Blow through the Red Districts

As soon as Horst Wessel had Storm 5 somewhat under control, he took it to the enemy. His combative nature urgently demanded activity. The first patrols in the Friedrichshain district, hitherto a firm possession of the Red Front, had a completely astounding effect on the enemy because of their incredible boldness. They could not believe that such a small force dared to appear against a superiority of more than twenty. Sneaky, cowardly attacks by crude reds on individual SA men were not uncommon. So far, no SA man had been seen in the dangerous area.

Horst Wessel asked little about that. He looked for his place where it was most dangerous. In individual groups or squads of two and three men on separate routes, the SA people of Storm 5 moved through Berlin in the evening as inconspicuously as possible towards their designated assembly point.

Suddenly a sharp whistle sounded through the streets or alleys, and the SA fighters, who were waiting in hiding everywhere, hurried over. The procession quickly got into order, and marched to the place where the enemy had gathered.

The Nazis' incursion into their very own territory initially leaves the reds speechless. Then the howls and wails start. A flood of the most savage insults pelts the united brown guard. But they stand firm and dutiful; so they endure the hail without challenging it with assaults. The supervising officer only waits for a physical attack, but nothing happens on the part of the Brownshirts. They obey the orders of their young leader with strict discipline. The angry Red Fronters must also curb their desire for violence if they do not want the meeting to be broken up.

Horst Wessel steps forward and speaks with the deliberate composure of an experienced popular speaker. But also with the cutting sharpness of a determined fighter, he hurls his sentences into the dully seething masses, without letting himself be distracted by the piercing looks of hatred from the enemies. His speech is at the same time a declaration of war against the insidious mob, which practices devious attacks on individual defenseless SA men as a kind of sport and even boasts of these dark, cowardly misdeeds. The tone in which the red press reports such inhuman maltreatment and manslaughter is so vile and cynical that every German must blush with shame at the fact that these shameful reports were published in German. The enemies grit their teeth with rage when Horst Wessel shouts at them in a piercing voice the threat that the SA is no longer willing to let the red terror of violence go unpunished. Harsh retribution is to be inflicted for the beating of an SA man, and every sly stab and every murder will now be met with bloody retribution. An eye for an eye, a tooth for a tooth! Thus Horst Wessel fearlessly hurls the threat of just retribution into the faces of his cowardly, dehumanized opponents.

They grumble and growl like treacherous predators, but dare not attack in the face of the Brownshirts' resolute stance. They know the power and force of Storm 5. Horst Wessel has achieved one thing: the red enemies have learned to fear him and his valiant storm. Too often in recent times have they been given samples of the courage, fearlessness, and bravery of this Storm 5, who is the most hated in their circles.

After Horst Wessel has thrown down the gauntlet to his opponents in a chivalrous manner, he and his bold band leave the pub, surrounded by the insults of the raging community. There are small riots in various places, beer glasses come flying, smash on the floor, even chairs are used as projectiles, but no one dares to engage man-to-man. One has learned to one's own detriment in the red camp in Friedrichshain that a powerful spirit, the spirit of this very young student, has entered the SA from Storm 5. This lowly rabble is much too cowardly for open combat.

Once outside, harsh commands resound. The storm troopers quickly organize themselves, as calmly as on the training ground, and march off at the same pace. The storm hymns of the youthful leader roar through the streets of the district—a stronghold of communism—sung out of a joyful feeling of strength. They sound like trumpets heralding a new battle, but also a new time of awakening for an urban area in which the sinister agitation is carrying out its shameful work of destruction on the German spirit.

In the red headquarters a storm of indignation raged and foamed because the hated, much weaker opponent, had dared to break into an uncontested area of the Red Front, to dispute their exclusive and violently-claimed right to the street.

But the red camp was even more outraged that the most capable members of the Red Front were now serving as loyal SA men in Storm 5. They did not have to search long for the cause: Horst Wessel's eloquence, in combination with his irreproachable attitude as a comrade and leader, opened the eyes of the lost and showed them the only right way.

This realization created a storm of hatred in the ranks of the enemy, which was directed against Horst Wessel, the young blond student from the Judenstraße. Horst Wessel was now the most hated and persecuted person in Berlin. He shared the fate of *Gauleiter* Dr. Goebbels, whom his loyal SA had only too often been able to save from the clutches of this treacherous vermin, sometimes by the skin of his teeth. The Rhinelander's bold, incisive language, the persuasive power of his speech was a stake in the flesh for the Berlin rulers of the Weimar system. In order to put him out of action, the mob was stirred up and the scum of the city set upon him.

Now they had to contend even with this brazen boy from the Jüdenstraße, who not only disintegrated and wore down the ranks of the Red Front through his power of speech, but even more so through his outrageously bold aggressiveness and his skilful leadership in the street fight! In the opinion of the Red Front leaders, it was even more urgent to get rid of him.

Thus it came about that danger lurked on Horst Wessel's every path, by day and by night. It was not a secret to him that they wanted to get rid of him; the signs were too obvious. But he was a soldier, a fighter for his people and a new Germany, so there was no backing down. Calm and full of confident courage, he continued his service. He faithfully remained at his post. Friendly but firm, he rejected well-intentioned warnings from his comrades. The right heroic spirit was alive in this young man, which made him continue on his way unflinchingly. It was not out of wantonness or careless recklessness that he braved the dangers with calm courage, but because a strong sense of duty that had penetrated deep into his being drove the young man.

Storm 5 Gets a Shawm Band

Horst Wessel's inventive mind was always on the lookout for ways and means to fight the enemy. He had often been annoyed when the tantalizing sound of the shawm band met his ear during communist parades. He knew the reds were proud of this garishly resounding defiant music, which they regarded as their sole means of advertising on the street.

Soon it was clear to Horst Wessel: his storm had to have a shawm band, no matter the cost. That was a good idea, but where would he get the instruments? It would cost money, and they didn't have any.

Once Horst had set his sights on something, he carried it through. His inventive mind solved even this difficult issue. By issuing small-value vouchers and other aids, he pushed the matter through, and one day his storm marched through the streets of Berlin with a shawm band at its head.

This, of course, caused great amazement in his own camp and even more so in the circles of the red Muscovites, who were seething with rage. But what could they do about it?

The brave musicians couldn't play right away, but the driving force of Horst Wessel soon succeeded in making the band able to. It was not difficult to learn how to play, and there were a number of people in the band who had previously played in the opposing band. The plan soon worked.

Night fell over Berlin. Lighting also flared up in the streets of the darkest, most disreputable parts of Berlin more sparsely, of course, than in the streets flooded with traffic. Dull, restrained, furtive, and shy, nightlife glided through crooked, sometimes narrow streets in this red quarter.

There—what is that? Are the communists moving again to the tantalizing sounds of their shawms, which make the good bourgeois feel sick to their stomachs? It must be so, because apart from the Red Front, no association dares to march into this area, where the red communists alone claim and exercise their rule.

But the shouts of "Berlin remains red!" "Heil Moscow!" and "Death to all fascists!" which otherwise roar threateningly up to the front of the houses at such marches, are not heard.

What's that? The melody is familiar—Nazi songs and Nazi marches blare in a high, fresh sound through the nocturnal quarters of the red headquarters, with Storm 5's shawm band in front!

Yes, it's them! The Nazis are marching in the middle of the night through the middle of the enemy camp, where until now no brown-shirted man was allowed to show himself, if he did not want to run the risk of being knocked down or sent round the corner by a slyly inflicted stab.

And now the storm marches in unison behind their hard-won and sacrificially fought-for shawm band, in orderly columns and at a steady pace. The echoing chant of their songs of comradeship, loyalty, and devotion to the German fatherland floats above the processions, thunderously filling the narrow streets and banging in the ears of the enemy.

This outrageously bold, challenging night-march through hitherto undisputed enemy territory arouses consternation and bewilderment among the enemy, who stare in horror and amazement at the procession. Then their rage rises to the top, and their wild, dirty drool pours out over the platoons marching along with proud calm. A veritable rat's tail of howling, hooting opponents, provided by the Berlin underworld, rolls behind them.

The enemy feels this bold night-march of the brown SA through his territory like a slap in the face.

The question is: who could have concocted this insulting plan?

Who, who, who? But only the one, that blond-haired student with the calm face, the steady eyes and the proud posture. Didn't you see him? He marched right behind the shawm band in front of Storm 5. Satan take them, him, the band, and the storm itself! This Horst Wessel is the soul of the whole thing, always inventing new means to loosen the power of the reds in the streets, in the meeting halls, and in the red associations. Many a person who seemed to belong with heart and soul to communism or Marxism was persuaded by his eloquence to join the brown army.

He, and always he, the young enthusiastic champion of a new empire, completely imbued with the great Führer's true ideals, confronted the red masses—who felt unassailable in their position of power—in a conspicuous position, causing damage and mischief.

His name ran from mouth to mouth around the red camp. A hissing, seething wave of hatred trailed behind his figure like a foaming wake from a proud ocean liner. Soon this hatred formed itself into a single thought of annihilation of all who belonged to the Red Front: he must be eliminated; he must fall.

But it was not only the broad mass of the communist supporters living in darkest Berlin who pursued the bright figure of the young *Sturmführer*, striding through the battlefields with proud, bold composure, with a vicious will to destroy him; the enemy leaders had also become aware of his activities, which were so tremendously harmful to them. The more his work progressed, the stronger the idea of his elimination became in the leadership circles of the opponents. They knew: Horst Wessel was worth an army.

Secretly, a shy army of cowardly murderous thoughts crept around the light path of the young National Socialist. He was not unaware of what was being planned against him, but undeterred, he continued to walk along as the leader of his Storm 5, with such cool boldness that it had an almost intimidating and spellbinding effect. Again and again came warnings from circles of friends, but he did not scoff at them; with a friendly word he smoothed them over with a firm sense of duty: "I stand at a post and hold out there, whatever may happen."

This nocturnal march into enemy territory was only the prelude to further attacks by the brown army of National Socialism, which smashed breach after breach into the fortifications of the red hordes.

The Trip to Pomerania

In places where it was necessary to raise the prestige of the brown SA and to introduce the ideas of National Socialism, the Berlin SA appeared to help the local storm troopers and to promote the good cause.

Thus, in the late autumn of 1928, a publicity drive was ordered to the Pomeranian town of Pasewalk. On trucks, eighty Berlin SA people drove through the sunlit countryside, swastika flags fluttering merrily in the wind above their heads.

Pasewalk was a place of remembrance due to a significant stay by the Führer. Here, in 1918, Adolf Hitler had sought healing in a military hospital from the burning eye pain that afflicted him after a fierce bombardment by English gas shells near Ypres. It was here that the sight in his eyes faded and a deep night enveloped him. The artistically inclined man, whose rich sense was enthusiastic about everything beautiful in nature and the environment, may have spent terrible days there, when the deep darkness surrounded him and he had to fear losing his eyesight. The debilitating darkness from without was joined by the darkness within; for the hour of destiny came upon the defeated Germany, the overthrow took place, and criminal elements overthrew the old empire that Bismarck had forged for eternity. This news shook the soldier who had fought four years for his fatherland with tears that had not wetted his eyes since the death of his kind mother.

For the Führer, the name Pasewalk was forever associated with the darkest hours of his existence.

And now trucks rolled along the light gray strips of country roads to spread and impart the liberating spirit of the man in the little town who had fought through hard days there as a desperate, blinded, field-gray soldier.

Bright luster flashed from the eyes of the SA people, and a proud sense of strength lifted their courage in the consciousness of belonging together with the many other like-minded people. Their fresh songs resounded euphorically in the Sunday calm of the sunny autumn day. The new Germany greeted the people in the villages through which the train passed with youthful voices.

With the confidence of victory of those who believe in a just cause, they sang to the hurrying villagers:

Noch ist die Freiheit nicht verloren,
Noch sind wir nicht so ganz besiegt,
In jedem Lied wird sie geboren,
Das aus der Brust der Lerche fliegt.
Sie rauscht uns zu im jungen Laube,
Im Strom, der durch die Felsen drängt,
Sie glüht im Purpursaft der Traube,
Der brennend seine Bande sprengt.

Laßt euch die Kette nicht bekümmern,
Die noch an eurem Arme klirrt.
Zwing-Uri liegt in Schutt und Trümmern,
Sobald ein Tell geboren wird.
Die blanke Kette ist für Toren,
Für freie Männer ist das Schwert!
Noch ist die Freiheit nicht verloren,
Solang ein Herz sie heiß begehrt!

Freedom is not yet lost,
Nor are we completely defeated,
Freedom is born in every song
That comes from the lark's breast.
It rushes to us in the small gardenhouse,
In the stream that flows through the rocks,
It glows in the purple juice of the grape,
That bursts through its shell with fire.

Let not the chain trouble you,
That still clatters on your arm.
Zwing-Uri lies in ruins,[20]
As soon as a Tell is born.[21]

---

[20] Zwing Uri is a ruined medieval castle in Switzerland.
[21] Tell refers to Wilhelm Tell, a character from the book with the same name by Friedrich Schiller. The book was finished in 1804.

The bright chain is for fools,
For free men is the sword!
Freedom is not yet lost,
As long as one heart desires it!

The Berlin SA was particularly fond of singing this song, as it was the favorite song of their doctor Joseph Goebbels. They loved him, they fought and suffered for him, and in him they worshipped the representative of the distant Führer, who hammered the pure doctrine into their hearts and minds with irresistible momentum.

But they also felt, while singing, the strong spirit that sounded from the words of the song, and a joy of hope shone through the souls of these people who were eager to fight. At such moments, these loyal Brownshirts were overcome by a Pentecostal spirit; they believed with all the strength of their fiery hearts in the victory of the good cause, and everything, everything else that life had to offer them: profession, position, and income, was indifferent to them. "*Laß fahren dahin*," as it says in the old "Luthertrutzkampflied"; for them only the fight and the commitment of one's own person were the ruling elements.

Adolf Hitler had to win with such troops, just as the great Frederick did at Leuthen, when his rough grenadiers sang spiritual morning songs.

So the journey continued with joyful, open-hearted singing until bright shouts of salvation blared out towards them and swastika flags waved in greeting.

With the Hitler-flag waving, the Pasewalk SA caught up with them in the old cavalry garrison town, through whose alleys the footsteps of spurred cuirassier boots once clanked. Right at the reception, the slogan was issued: "Beware—trouble!"

On hearing of the advertising day that the Nazis wanted to hold in Pasewalk, the Red Front had immediately ordered reinforcements from Berlin to the small town, in mighty numbers. They had already arrived by train in the morning. The clashes seemed inevitable.

The SA columns entered Pasewalk to the sound of fresh marching music. The rousing rhythm of their songs, infused with spiritual faith, rose up in a roar and echoed in the narrow streets or roared strongly and powerfully across the squares. Trivial friction and light banter did not disturb the procession and did not stop it in its tight posture.

Everything seemed to go well.

After the procession, the trucks remained behind under the care of a small guard force. The other participants marched to the shooting club, where rations were waiting for them.

But the peace was short-lived. From somewhere, news suddenly drove into the pub that the Red Front had attacked the wagons at the market and that the guard was in a completely hopeless battle with superior enemy forces.

All the men abandoned their food and wanted to storm off. But the *Sturmführer's* order confined them to their places. He alone let the soup get cold and went out with two men on reconnaissance. Unfortunately, the rumor was confirmed, the battle had broken out, and the situation of the guard was an extremely dangerous one.

Fiedler, from Storm 1, stood high up on one of the wagons with his pistol cocked, surrounded by a few hundred communists, banging and rattling all around him.

Albert Sprengel, the *Sturmführer*, also got into a bad situation because his pistol failed. But he managed to save himself when a detachment of *Landjäger* with raised sabers cleared the market square.[22] He hid in an entryway, let them pass, and then ran off to cover, after quickly making sure that his comrades had also saved their skins.

But no sooner had everyone gathered there than the Red Front moved in and surrounded the building.

By the way the reds proceeded, using every possible cover, those trapped immediately recognized that Berlin communists, used to fighting, were carrying out the task.

"They're very clever," said Fiedler. "Scherlinski's probably in on it."

"It doesn't matter whether it's him or Schlageter; we'll send them home with battered heads," growled Sprengel. The name of the freedom fighter Schlageter, who had been shot by the French on the Golzheimer *Heide* near Düsseldorf, had been adopted by the communists as a mockery of one their enemies.

Sprengel immediately grasped the situation. He ordered that all available and usable material be brought in and used to build a

---

[22] A *Landjäger* is a type of sausage. Here it is being used to refer to mounted police, who are being perceived as stiff, like the sausages.

defense force. The SA went to work with great enthusiasm and erected a barricade of benches, chairs, barrels, shutters, and beams. The swastika banner fluttered above this barricade. They were determined to defend themselves here.

The wild attackers tightened their circle around the group. With pistols blazing, they closed in on the brave SA squad. There were a few wounded, who were given the only first aid kits, and they continued to fight with the firm resolve not to be driven out.

Suddenly, however, *Tschakos* appeared[23]; *Landjäger* moved in with the Schutzpolizei.[24] There was a not very violent exchange of bullets between the approaching police force and the communists, and then the red attackers quickly disappeared.

Then the police pounced on the Hitler-activists, wanting to quickly root out the brown nest. But *Sturmführer* Sprengel would never dream of surrendering with his men. How? Had he built the barricade for this purpose, only to see his people crawl out from behind it like wet poodles? No, nothing could be done! He laughed in the face of the police officer demanding surrender. No one moved from his post and the banging continued. The Greencoats thought that was a bit funny.[25] After some hesitation, they fired too.

A mighty noise in the corner of the hall drew Sprengel's attention. Some of his men were busily smashing a huge crate, the boards flying about. And what did it reveal? A new, flashing gun. "Hooray, a cannon!" roared the finders of the heaven-sent ordnance. A great mood had seized them. They tore open the gate and pushed the cannon out. The wheels rolled over the planks with a dull roar and the tail of the gun carriage came crashing down.

This went beyond what the good Landjäger had in mind. They wanted to take part in a harmless skirmish, in which they had little fun and little desire, but they did not want to make any closer acquaintance with grenades and shrapnel, much less with cartridges, the dreaded close-range projectile of field artillery. They gave thanks and withdrew as quickly as possible. The Landjäger disappeared from the immediate vicinity.

And the winners? They cheered, but then they laughed like never

---

[23] *Tschako* means shako, a type of tall, cylindrical military hat.
[24] Protection-police
[25] "Greencoats" (*Grünröcken*) refers to the Landjäger, and was a pejorative term for the rural police forces in Germany. The term refers to their green uniform.

before in their lives. The Pasewalk SA comrades quickly informed them of the find. The famous field cannon had been stuck in its hiding place for several years now, from which it had now been freed so suddenly. Shyly, its shiny barrel peeked out into the autumn sunshine. It had come there as a gift to the traditional Pasewalk cuirassiers' association and was to be erected somewhere in memory of thunderous battles. Where? Well, in the usual German discord, the responsible authorities could not agree on this, and so the well-behaved gun waited in its wooden prison for the day when the sun would once again produce glaring streaks of light on the bright barrel. The reds and a resourceful SA man had seen to that.

But how soon the joy of discovery came to an end! The mayor of Pasewalk was sweating bullets on that memorable day; he had no desire to have his Sunday rest disturbed any longer. The red communist rabble was already a very dangerous and difficult company to deal with, but these nasty SA devils could make a good city official's heart ache. Now it was high time to call in the Reichswehr, which had long since been on standby in the barracks. They would deliver one hell of a punishment. At the mere thought of it, the good mayor felt goose bumps running down his spine at high speed.

The Reichswehr moved in, led by a *Rittmeister*.[26] A single glance at the riders armed with carbines and hand grenades showed that any further resistance was unreasonable. What were they going to do about it with a few guns?

To the *Rittmeister's* demand to surrender, Sprengel replied, "to the Reichswehr—immediately!"

But there was still a catch for the storm troopers. Weapons must not be found on them, or else they were in trouble.

But Sprengel knew what to do.

"Horst, you act as my adjutant here! Quickly collect all the firearms and hand them over to us!" In a few minutes the guns were collected, and the *Sturmführer* and his newly appointed adjutant stowed them under their blouses and shirts, so that they resembled walking arsenals. They looked a little informal, but so be it.

"SA, line up!" commanded Sprengel, and already forty Pasewalk and eighty Berlin SA people were standing there, lined up in a

---

[26] A *Rittmeister* is a cavalry officer.

straight line. Sprengel, always followed by Horst, reported to the *Rittmeister* and asked that his men be searched for weapons.

This was done quite thoroughly. Every SA man was patted down and the house searched. Only the *Sturmführer* and his adjutant remained untouched. Nothing was found.

"Hmm, you don't have any weapons," the *Rittmeister* noted and added, "What are you actually shooting with? Two *Landjäger* got wounded."

Sprengel raised his shoulders expressively, but could not refrain from answering, "With cannons without a breech."

The cannon was missing this main part, without which it was just a piece of jewelry.

The captain grinned, inwardly of course, but Albert Sprengel could see it in the slight itch of his nostrils and the merry twinkle in his eyes.

Then the officer said to Albert, "You've got tough guys, but they're skinny, skinny as beanstalks, all of them without exception. Only you two, the young man and you, have mighty bellies—and a chest size that is well worth seeing. Only the way that the fat is distributed on your bodies is a bit strange. You must be all right, eh?"

Sprengel answered with a tight posture, "Yes, Herr Rittmeister! Brisk living in the SA!"

A smile crossed the officer's face. "I'm very pleased," he says happily, and then demands in an official tone that the Berlin SA leave immediately in their trucks, which Sprengel certainly agrees to. At this, the *Rittmeister* allows himself to be shown around their defensive positions. At the sight of the quickly erected entrenchment, he stops and examines the construction with an expert eye.

When he asked who had built the barricade, Sprengel explained that the reds, who were coming at them from all sides, had forced them to erect these defenses.

"It's not bad—your barricade was built in an artistic way, well done! What is your name?"

"Albert Sprengel, Standard 4, Storm 1, Berlin, Herr Rittmeister!" replied the interrogated man.

The *Rittmeister's* right hand went to the brim of his cap in greeting. "I am pleased to have met you. Well, make sure you get home, and—

goodbye, Barrikadenalbert!"[27]

Boom! Sprengel now had a nickname that would stick with him for all time.

Homeward they went, after the adventure with a sour beginning and a cheerful ending. But there was an epilogue. Sprengel had returned to Berlin with the wounded and the pistols by train, because he rightly feared that their caring acquaintances from Alexanderplatz would give them an attentive reception. A sure scent told him that a reception committee from the police headquarters was waiting for them at Alexanderplatz or at the Stettin railway station, and so he got off the train with his men at Gesundbrunnen and they all made it home unchallenged.

Those returning home by truck were not so lucky. They were hauled off and once again given free quarters in the "Alex," as they called the police headquarters on Alexanderplatz in their abbreviated dialect. Horst Wessel and his comrade Fiedler were among them.

The matter took the usual course. Arrested—interrogated—released. That was part of the business, and no SA man thought anything of it. They took the few days in custody like morning and evening. Horst was far too inwardly connected with the movement and his comrades to think otherwise. He was only embarrassed because of his mother. For the sensitive woman, this arrest by the guardians of public safety always had something hurtful about it. In her good middle-class mind, she suffered greatly at the thought of her boy being taken to that place where the scum of the street who had fallen foul of the law was dumped. But never a word of rebuke or even regret crossed her lips; her trust in her boy was too firmly established for that.

Horst Wessel accepted the days of imprisonment like an unavoidable sacrifice. He saw an act of violation on the part of the ruling power in these arrests, which he felt like a provocation. All the more reason to fight the men from whom it emanated.

But the enforced stay in the prison cells was also a gain for Horst and the movement he represented in other respects. The involuntary leisure gave him the most beautiful opportunity to reflect on the struggle for German renewal and the reawakening of national solidarity. In the silence of the prison cell, many a poem was written

---

[27] Barricades-Albert

that bore witness to Horst Wessel's high flight of thought, whose thinking was completely permeated by the spirit of national renewal. A comparison with another poet of liberty inevitably forces itself upon us: Theodor Körner and Horst Wessel. In these two men, German to the core, the same feelings of honest hatred and anger against the tyrannical oppressors of the German people are alive. Both stand in the ranks of the liberating struggle movement. Both inflame the freedom-fighters with their songs of defiance. While the wounded Theodor Körner wrote down his songs cheering the nation on the bed of pain, the SA man Horst Wessel composed his rousing battle songs behind barred prison walls. The same flame of devoted love for the Fatherland blazed in these two poets, igniting in the minds of thousands of German brothers the will to liberate themselves from the disgraceful yoke of tyranny.

What stands out clearly and distinctly for us here is the realization of how the spiritual spark from Horst Wessel's world of thought jumps over to the masses and spreads out in fruitful circles.

Publicity Trip to Frankfurt on the Oder

In order to spread the idea of the power and inner strength of National Socialism in the Reich and especially in the larger cities, the regional leadership had arranged a promotional trip to Frankfurt on the Oder by the Berlin and other SA standards. Late one fine May evening Standard 4, to which Horst Wessel's storm belonged, gathered in Hoppegarten. After a two-hour night-march, the Brown-shirts were loaded into trucks and taken to their destination. With satisfaction, *Staf*[28] Breuer noticed that only a few of his crew were missing. And these few had—unfortunately—valid excuses for their absence. Some were ill, others were in jail, and one had been beaten up by communists the day before and was seriously injured.

They arrived in Trebbin in the fresh cool May morning, where they were given breakfast by a friendly landowner.

Then they marched to the assembly point, which was not far from the town of Frankfurt. There the standards met and formed a stately procession, which must have been impressive. The people of

---

[28] Abbreviation for *Standartenführer*

Frankfurt were to see for themselves what the brown SA actually was and what it meant.

The procession set off and marched in impeccable order through all the districts of the city. It was a joy. Courage, confidence, and faith in the ideals they had chosen for themselves as Germans shone from the eyes and expressions of the brave Brownshirts during this march through the streets of Frankfurt. The many hundreds marched through the streets in steady step with the roaring sound of rousing songs above the columns.

The tight order that prevailed in all the storm squadrons must have left a pleasant impression. In order not to call this into question and not to give any opportunity for jostling, which could easily degenerate into brawls, the *OSAF* had given counter-orders: "No one is to leave the hall and the garden of the headquarters, which are a little out of the way."

However, after a short time, word reached the leaders that a squad of SA men had been involved in a scuffle with communist members, which was threatening to escalate. Firearms were used by both sides. The police force was unable to break up the parties.

This was bad news that could ruin the exquisite impression created by the publicity stunt.

The *OSAF* immediately summoned his staff to investigate the matter and advise appropriate action. It soon turned out that crews from Storm 1 had gone into the city to look around before the order was announced. On their peaceful stroll, they had then come across the reds, and after a brief exchange of words, the scuffle began.

For the *OSAF*, the story became most unpleasant. He had vouched to the authorities for peace and order, and now there were disturbances. He knew from experience that it was not easy to break up such a fight. It had to be Storm 1 to be involved in this nasty business. When the people of the other storm detachments of Standard 4 learned that Storm 1 had joined hands with the reds inside the city, there was nothing to stop them from rushing to the aid of their comrades. The troops of Standard 4 hung together like glue; they would strike like spirits of hell, and the mess would be even bigger. But who should he send without the good boys feeling left behind?

Good advice was expensive. By chance, his eye caught a youthful face. A bright glow passed over his worried face.

"*Sturmführer* 5!" his voice rang through the hall. Horst Wessel came forward and was ordered to get Storm 1, which was in combat with members of the Red Front, out of the city at all costs. He was not given any specific orders on how to carry them out; he was to act at his own discretion and according to the circumstances he found.

Storm 5 arrived. These were guys Wessel could rely on. They set off running, on detours and through huddled crowds to the market.

The *OSAF* looked after the departing men and muttered to himself, "If anyone can do it, it's Wessel. I don't know of any other *Sturmführer* who could handle this nasty business with the same skill as Horst."

The young *Sturmführer* had earned such trust from the top leadership.

Things looked bad at the market.

Storm 1 had been forced by the huge mass into the entrance of a side alley. Maybe there was an opportunity to get out of the way here, but none of the storm troopers wanted to know about it, especially their *Sturmführer*, Barrikadenalbert. He was quite a guy, a tough character. He certainly didn't desert. What—those from Storm 1, Standard 4, were supposed to run away, cowardly, from that Frankfurt communist scum? There could be no such thing!

Horst Wessel quickly looked over the situation.

Over there at the corner of the square, where the masses were pushing and shoving, Storm 1 was in an almost hopeless fight. Those under Barrikadenalbert were already charging at the reds, but in the long run, they would not have been able to stand up to such a superior force.

He will beat them out with his famous Storm 5. Between them and the fighting comrades an excited crowd surges, hooting and hollering with rage. But they are not Berlin Red Front members after all, and he has his storm troop behind him. Storm 5 will show them.

And he showed the people of Frankfurt what he could do. No sooner was the order given to dig in than the storm troopers, following their leader, threw themselves into the fray with lightning speed. Like an iron, cutting axe, they furrowed the raging crowd, which howled and pushed aside to avoid the hard boxing blows of Storm 5.

In an incredibly short time they had reached the scene of the battle. The street was quickly cleared of the completely surprised communists, who did not know what was happening to them.

Sturmführer Albert Sprengel was delighted to see the Brownshirts appear in the melee. He caught his breath and shouted his "Sieg Heil!" to the rescuers in a hoarse voice, while blood ran down his battered face and dripped onto his torn brown shirt.

"Now let's go—hit them hard!" he shouted in a newly-inflamed fighting spirit, cheering on his men. He was already rushing forward when he hit the ground. Someone had put his foot down.

Furious, he jumped up, ready to punch the culprit in the teeth, when he found himself face to face with Horst Wessel.

"What the hell! Come on, this is where the story really starts to get fun!" he shouted at the comrade.

At Horst Wessel's wave, two comrades grabbed Barrikadenalbert by the arms. That was more than just fun. He was dying to pay back the enemy with more blows, and they wanted to stop him! He could do nothing!

He tried to free himself by force. Strong as a bear, he shook off the comrades holding him, but then the *Sturmführer* 5 caught him by the hook. A firm grip—a swing—and the stunned Barrikadenalbert sat with his backside against the ground, staring dumbfounded at his friend.

"Hey, are you all crazy?" he snapped, gasping for breath.

"Just come along, Albert," Wessel said calmly. "Call your people together; it's no use; you must obey. The show is over—orders from the *OSAF*!"

Confused, they look at each other, standing there, ready to get going with the reinforcements they had received. The order stunned them—but—order from the *OSAF*—for crying out loud—no one dared make a sound.

Barrikadenalbert may have had the biggest mouth in the whole of Standard 4, but he doesn't complain. Orders are orders, so one has to obey. "What a pity, what a pity," he thinks as he groans and stands up. "We were so well on our way and would have beaten up those Frankfurt red brutes so that the pieces would have flown about!" There now stands his famous Storm 1, heads bowed, hearts full of combativeness. Some have received a bloody lesson. Anger and rage boil within them, but there is only one thing to do here: obey. Orders from the *OSAF*—that's enough.

The column is formed and marches off at full speed to the safe house.

Horst Wessel reports, "Order executed!"

The bright eyes of the *OSAF* shine at the young student. "Good, Wessel! I knew you'd make it!"

Later, when they talked about the trip to Frankfurt, Barrikadenalbert would grimace as if he had drunk vinegar. In his opinion, the day was an unfortunate one for the Zackig Standard, but it had nevertheless proved by its obedience that strict manly discipline prevailed in the troop, and that was also praiseworthy.

Raise the Flags

The SA is on guard duty at the Busch Circus. It is the first time that they are on duty at a meeting that does not promote the Hitler movement. The Nationale Hilfe had called this meeting to protest against the shameful sentences of a black-red-gold judiciary, which had condemned men who loved their German fatherland with all the ardor of their feelings to death and dishonorable prison sentences. These men, driven by the patriotism of action, were scornfully shouted out and insulted as "Feme murderers." Everyone that felt a spark of national spirit and did not cowardly hide its opinion from the power clique found his way to the meeting place.

Standard 4 stood lined up on Monbijou Square. Loud commands rang out, and the storm troopers marched off in steady step. Curious citizens watched the march with somewhat ambivalent feelings. In the silence of their bourgeois souls they hoped that these sturdy brown boys would drive the red Bolshevists in Germany out and save their own bourgeois comfort from the bloody lust for power of the communists. But, yes, there was a "but" behind this wish: they themselves, these belligerent Brownshirts, were also street fighters and yet so often disturbed the peace and quiet, precisely that peace and quiet which the good, hard-working bourgeois considers to be the greatest good on earth. These good, simple people, confined in a venerable circle of thought, resisted the hard realization that only the most ruthless violence could conquer the threatening flood of violence of Bolshevism. This was the only way to save Germany from falling into the communist abyss.

Staf 4 suddenly listened, and with him, the comrades of the other storms. What was that song Storm 5 was singing? A new one, never heard before, whose melodious rhythm attracted the attention of the listeners to a great extent. There it was again—first and foremost Storm 5 with its youthful leader, from whose deep sensibilities the best marching songs emerged as if from an inexhaustible source of German national feeling.

For the first time, during the roaring march of the SA columns, it roared up to the sky, the "Horst Wessel Song":

Die Fahnen hoch! Die Reihen dicht geschlossen!
SA marschiert mit ruhig-festem Schritt.
Kameraden, die Rotfront und Reaktion erschossen,
Marschiern im Geist in unsern Reihen mit.

Raise the flag! The ranks tightly closed!
The SA marches with calm, steady step.
Comrades shot by Red Front and reactionaries
March in spirit within our ranks.

How it ignited! Entirely under the spell of this song and its heart-wrenching melody, the columns listened as it was time to continue:

Die Straße frei den braunen Bataillonen!
Die Straße frei dem Sturmabteilungsmann!
Es schaun aufs Hakenkreuz voll Hoffnung schon Millionen,
Der Tag der Freiheit und für Brot bricht an.

Clear the streets for the brown battalions,
Clear the streets for the Sturmabteilung man!
Millions are looking upon the swastikas full of hope,
The day of freedom and of bread dawns!

Moved by the clarity with which the deep sense of vocation and the essence of the SA army was poetically expressed in these few lines, the marchers eagerly awaited the continuation:

Zum letztenmal wird nun Appell geblasen!
Zum Kampfe stehn wir alle schon bereit.
Bald flattern Hitlerfahnen über allen Straßen;
Die Knechtschaft dauert nur noch kurze Zeit!

For the last time, the call to arms resounds!
For the fight, we all stand prepared!
Already Hitler's banners fly over all the streets.
The time of bondage will last but a little while now!

The words of this stanza had an effect on the comrades of the valiant storm like a fanfare signal calling on those who were advancing victoriously in a hard struggle to make a final onslaught, calling on all their strength.

The song of the SA had been created and was sung by the whole army of the Brownshirts with the enthusiasm it kindled in them. No other song like it characterized the nature and tasks of the SA in the struggle of the National Socialist movement as clearly and sharply as the "Horst Wessel Song."

Now the brown freedom fighters had their storm hymn!

Because Horst Wessel was completely absorbed in the spirit of the Führer in mind and body, in will and feeling, he was also able to bring it to life in this song and convey it to the comrades of the entire SA in Germany with his brilliant wordplay. In this song, the young hero's collected mental strength, focused on one high goal, comes across to us in clear form.

The grueling orderly service in the overcrowded Busch Circus began. With self-sacrificing zeal, the SA ensured the undisturbed accommodation of the many thousands in the mighty hall.

After the speech, spotlights projected messages and protests against the disgraceful verdict on the wall. Most of them elicited jubilant approval, which was expressed in roaring shouts. But once, indignant opposition arose: Mahraun's letter was not applauded. He, the former *Freikorps* leader and creator of the Young German Order, had entered into an alliance with the state party, had turned to the black-red-gold camp, and thus excluded himself from the ranks of the national movement. A humiliated bunch of misguided German youth: that is how the Young Germans with their Maltese cross ensign left the meeting, which turned into a massive rally. At the end, the *"Deutschlandlied"* roared through the wide space, its powerful echo again awakening the longing for the united Fatherland in the hearts of the thousands.

The SA had strictly obeyed the orders that they had received and refrained from any protest: a fine demonstration of the strictest discipline. And when they had sung along to the *"Deutschlandlied"* with their arms raised high, the chorus of *"Deutschland erwache!"*— the National Socialist cry of defiance and struggle—rolled out over the crowd of thousands. It proclaimed the dawning of a new day, and evoked hope in the beaten hearts of all nationally-minded German men and women.

But the battle was far from over. It smoldered here and blazed there, became more and more fierce, more bitter, and claimed victims.

On the way home, Truppführer Sprengel asked about the new song, as he immediately suspected Horst to be the poet. Wessel gave him a copy and replied to the question of when he had written the famous poem that he had written it down on the memorable journey to Frankfurt: "Right after I picked you up together with your people, my dear Albert."

Barrikadenalbert growls a little to himself, because he doesn't like to remember that day. Grumpily he adds, "I really did not like you back there, the way you held me back when I really wanted to get going. But I have long since changed my mind. The mere act of punching—well, it's not much of an art. But in the face of such a great hostile mass, to knock the comrades out of the seething mess, to take the quarrelsome ones by the scruff of the neck and leave with them as ordered, that's a whole lot more. There's something about it. No one can imitate you that easily!"

Horst modestly deflects, but Sprengel continues, "Don't talk back; it's true. The *OSAF* knew that too; that's why he gave you the job. Listen, I've always thought you were quite a guy, but only since Frankfurt have I known what else you've got in you. You'll make your way, and it will lead high up."

Thinking about it, Horst Wessel replied, "So that's your opinion? Well, I am different from you; I also feel it very strongly sometimes. I also see the way—not always clearly, but I will go it; I will do what my conscience drives me to do, and I will stand where my duty as a German points me. One thing is clear to me, Albert: with the courage to sacrifice and the will to give blood and life, it is not done alone.

The Führer demands more."

"Even more?" asked Albert Sprengel.

"Yes, many other things; I cannot express it more precisely in words, but that we must commit ourselves with all of our spirit, with all of our will, and with all of our strength, if we want to lift Germany up to a new elevation, of that I am convinced!"

Horst Wessel acted according to these words until fate overtook him.

The Terror of the East

The blond student from the Jüdenstraße repeatedly led his tried and tested Storm 5 into closed attacks against the Red Front and smashed it at many important points. It became fragile.

But it was not only on the streets that the brown storm troopers advanced and held their ground; they also penetrated into the very bowels of the Communist Party. Horst, in particular, worked tirelessly to reduce the number of members in the enemy camp. The loss of the converts counted double because it meant an increase for the SA and the movement itself.

Horst Wessel's successes increasingly drew the attention of the red leaders to him, who by word and deed was inflicting a serious loss on their power.

This had to be stopped. What was the use of a single SA man being knocked to the ground or bleeding to death by an insidious knife thrust in the dark nooks and crannies of the night? It was a matter of hitting the leaders.

And one of the most dangerous was this pastor's son from the Jüdenstraße. The fact that he still carried his healthy bones freely through the streets of Berlin was felt almost as a disgrace in the opposing camp.

Both fighting parties were informed about everything that was going on in the other party. Thus it was known in the red headquarters that Horst Wessel did not heed the well-meant warnings of his superiors and comrades. It was also known that the faithful watched over the safety of their *Sturmführer* with the loyal love of comradeship that was alive and active in Storm 5. But they were also only too well-aware that this protection could only be a highly inadequate one, given the carefree manner in which Horst

Wessel moved about the streets of Berlin.

He had to be cleared away; that was certain!

Thus dark shadows, summoned by vengeful spirits, loomed over the life of the bright German youth in the brown shirt. With the clear-headed calm that comes from the consciousness of honest duty, Horst Wessel continued on his way to Germany's salvation, unconcerned about the dark plans of the brood of envious people.

Tired, he returned home one night from security duty after drinking a glass of beer with his comrade Fiedler. His way led him through Prenzlauer Straße. Near a pub called "Mexico," he was startled out of his quiet thoughts by a loud noise. One of those nasty scandalous scenes, which were a common occurrence in certain areas of Berlin, caught his attention. A rough guy was maltreating a girl in a completely inhuman way, while a mob of half-drunk onlookers, standing around the entrance of the bar, were happily jeering and watching the crude act of violence.

Horst Wessel was filled with indignation at the disgraceful action. He did not think about the fact that he was in the sphere of influence of his enemies, who were only waiting for an opportunity to attack him. There was a person, a German girl, a fellow citizen in distress, in need of his help; there was no thinking or careful weighing of the circumstances; he had to intervene.

Quickly he stepped up and gave the savage brute a few rough swings, which caused him to let go of his victim and quickly disappear into the darkness of the street.

Whimpering, the girl raised her bloodied face to her rescuer. Deep hopelessness spoke from the tired looks of the maltreated.

Horst Wessel was not the kind of person who would now leave the afflicted creature to her uncertain fate. He sent the girl to the washroom to clean herself while he waited for her in the restaurant. And when, after a short time, she sat opposite him, he was startled by the pale gray color of her face. *She must never have gone beyond the softness of the stone desert of Berlin and doesn't know how good free air and bright sunshine feel*, he must have thought.

Then he inquired about the circumstances. What he heard there in dry, simple words shocked him. And yet it was a reflection of the fate of thousands of young unemployed girls in the big city. Oh, he couldn't help them all! This one, whom he had snatched from the fists of a brutal man, was sitting in front of him and looking at him with half-fearful, half-indifferent looks. She no longer seemed to believe in a favorable change in her life.

He asked where she lived. She had no place to live, but sometimes slept with pitying friends or on some bench.

This struck a chord in the young fighter for Germany's liberation. A young creature of his own blood, a German, did not know where to lay her head to rest, and was exposed to all the rough jolts of a rough city life with no prospect of support or assistance. At this thought, which arose in his merciful soul, his decision was already made.

His hand went into his pocket, pulled out the purse, and the money inside went into the girl's trembling hands. His grandmother had given him the sum for a little trip. A summer trip! The girl there with the bloodless face needed it more; she could use it to build up a start to a new and proper life. Otherwise she was lost, possibly even drowned, in the swamp of the big city. No, he could not take that onto his conscience.

The trembling hands of the recipient held the money tightly. She said that she had learned to tailor and now wanted to pay her debts with part of the money. Then she would have enough left for a start. Ah—she wanted to get up already. Once she had a proper apartment again, she would get a job.

As she asserted this so simply and earnestly, Horst realized that she felt compelled to assure him that he had not addressed his gift to anyone unworthy.

When he asked her if she had anyone to look after her and if she did not belong to any association, she explained that she had no close relatives. She was a member of the Alliance of Red Women and Girls, but with a hopeless shrug of the shoulders she remained silent.

Horst Wessel nodded, knowing that this association was only concerned with the political activities of its members; it was completely indifferent to their welfare and concerns.

When he asked her what her name was, she only told him that it was Erna. With a look of shy gratitude she said goodbye to her savior, not daring to shake his hand.

Horst Wessel looked at the poor figure, pondering. Fate, or rather God's providence, had brought this miserable creature into his path, and he had been able to help the poorest. But how many thousands might have fallen to the same fate, without a kindly care sending them a support. Oh, there was much misfortune and misery in the world that urgently needed to be remedied. If only the right national solidarity could be established through German National Socialism, then things would get better. These poor people were nothing more than political fighting material for the street terror in the hands of these greedy red party leaders. Whether they suffered mentally or physically, or perished, it did not matter to them. If only the good cause had won, then the lot of these unfortunate community members would also be improved.

The warm-hearted student was deeply moved by the experience. Suddenly, a mocking voice snapped him out of his brooding and reverie.

"That was a fine little play of yours! You're definitely out of the money. But don't think it's going to help!"

"Well—and what do you care?" asked Horst calmly.

"No, nothing at all! What's that girl to me? I don't know anything about the pathetic thing more than you do, Wessel—don't you know me?" the other asked with a smile.

"I've certainly seen you before, but I don't know where and under what circumstances," Horst said, taking a closer look at the stranger.

"I'll help you out. It was in the Alex last autumn—at the interrogation because of the fireworks at the island bridge. In the lobby. You negotiated with Barrikadenalbert and then came to us, offered us Red Front members some of your sandwiches as well," the other recalled.

"Ah, now I'm getting the picture. That I went over to you had only the purpose of diverting the attention of the *Schupo* men from my comrades," Horst explained.[29]

"I knew that right away, but the sandwiches tasted great. After twenty hours in jail, you start to work up an appetite. My name is Roß, Camillo Roß, so you know."

"Pleased to meet you in person," replied the young National Socialist. He knew this Red Front member. He was a shrewd fellow. "If you want an answer—to all questions—I am at your disposal. I've already been able to convince many a person from your camp."

"It's not unknown to me, and it's not pleasant either. We want to play with our cards on the table, Wessel. You and I are both too

---

[29] *Schupo* is short for *Schutzpolizei*, and here refers to police officers.

imbued with the ideology for which we each advocate, for one to pull the other over to him. What is the use of saying much more about it? Something else prompts me to talk to you. You're a decent man, Wessel. I saw how you helped the girl out of the gutter out of pure humanity. Well, to put it briefly, I want to warn you!"

Horst looked at the red man, puzzled at first, then he replied with a laugh, "You, of all people? That's quite something new!"

"It doesn't matter whether it's new or not. You know that there are honest guys here too, and that's who you're aiming at when you speak at our meetings. You know how to steal the best elements away from us. With the others, the followers from the masses, there is no danger. They are much too lazy to think and fall for your bait. It's always the best boys of the Red Front who you talk into your SA, and we've looked at that long enough now. It's time to put an end to it."

"So? As far as I'm concerned, it's just about to start!" exclaimed Horst Wessel. "I intend to put the brown shirt on many of you."

"Listen, Wessel," the communist urgently admonished, "be satisfied with the success here. Your Storm 5 is a fine thing; it can be seen in an area where not so long ago no Brownshirt was to be seen and where no Nazi dared to go. You will understand that we look down on the matter and wish you to hell. That's why I advise you to look around for another district where you can work just as well— Berlin isn't a village."

"I'd like to know why you're giving me such good advice," was Wessel's reply.

"I can explain; it's simple enough," Camillo Roß replied with an approving nod. "We cannot and must not tolerate your rummaging here in our firmest district any longer. If you take my advice and voluntarily resign from this now-dangerous territory for you, so much the better for you and for us. We are not such that we do not appreciate an honest opponent when he is—well, when he is just such a figure as you, Wessel. Be reasonable."

"Well, what happens if I'm not?"

"Then you force us to use other, more radical means, because you have to go, that's for sure," Camillo Roß replied briefly and firmly.

"Well, there's nothing to be said about that; the answer is clear, and at least I know what to expect every day, and even more so at night. . . . Man, you pretend to know me, can you seriously imagine that I could ever abandon my comrades of Storm 5?"

"After all, it's up to you what you can and can't do," Roß grumbled. More animatedly, he continued, "You must come to the conclusion one day that you, the student and Corps member, never, ever belonged to the people. You are gifted, surely you want to occupy an outstanding position in life one day; you come from a middle-class parish home, of all places; the hour will come when you realize that you have gone astray, and then you will see the gap that separates you, the Corps student, from the proletarian people!"

"Gap? I see no such thing!" exclaimed Horst Wessel with conviction. "There are and should be no more proletarians in Germany, but only community members who, welded together by fortune and misfortune into a national body, go their way together. But you only fight for one class at the expense of the others. How can a national whole thrive?"

"Let's not argue about it. One thing is certain for me: you, with your sharp mind and your great talents, will never belong to the lowest class of people, nor will you attract the stupid mass of proles to you, because you, as an educated man, know nothing about the life of the masses," Camillo Roß said harshly, and then left the table.

Horst Wessel looked at him, concerned. The conversation had excited him more deeply than he had first thought. Not because of the threat hidden in the warning; that could not touch Wessel particularly deeply, because he was aware of the dangers that surrounded him. But what Roß, a decent enemy by the way, had told him, that was what was drilling into him. He had noticed very well that Roß had shaken hands with some of the boys loitering at the door as they left, but not with him—Wessel. The poor girl had also withdrawn her hand halfway. Was he still a stranger in the lowest social classes, who was met with an unjustified, even insulting mistrust? It was a shocking realization for this young man to have to tell himself that he, who was attached to people from the lower classes with a love that came from a compassionate heart, was still not considered a brother.

This raged in him like a slowly smoldering fire. But his strong spirit did not slacken in useless brooding; he was a man of action through and through and wanted to have certainty at all costs. That is why he made a decision, boldly and quickly, as he did everything: he wanted to go to the masses themselves, to descend into their circles of life, to become one of them, in order to understand them completely and to be able to put Hitler's doctrine of socialism into practice for all members of the people and to prove it.

HORST WESSEL THE WORKER

Farewell to the Old Life

Horst Wessel packed up his seven things to leave his parents' apartment in the Jüdenstraße and descend into the world of the fourth class, to experience its life for himself—as a worker.

The mother joined them. She was happy because she thought her boy finally wanted to relax and take a trip somewhere in the wide, beautiful country. Her motherly care awoke immediately, and she prepared some bread for him and fetched another bottle of wine.

"Inge and Werner will be back from the university soon, and then we'll take you to the station together, my boy," said the kind woman with joy. She knew how exhausting the last few weeks had been for Horst and that he desperately needed a rest. Inge and Werner, Horst's younger siblings, were in the middle of their studies. Werner also belonged to the SA and was a loyal member of the brown storm troopers. He saw in his brother a shining example. The always-cheerful Inge also clung to her hardworking brother with warm affection.

"Where do you want to go?" asked Mrs. Wessel.

"Mother, I don't want to deceive you. It's not my intention to go on a journey; I really don't have time for that now. I'm leaving you to rent a apartment somewhere in the working district and live there. I want to become a worker, to get to know the life of the German worker down to the last emotion," Horst replied.

"Become a worker? But—isn't it enough, if you work within the framework assigned to you and study diligently, to become a capable person who will one day occupy a respectable position?" said the worried woman.

"No, it is not that. I want to work with my hands like the many thousands, I want to get tired like them, and I want to have to live from the yield of this work of mine; to put it bluntly, I want to experience the existence of a lowly worker first-hand," he explained firmly and calmly.

"And that's why you want to leave us?"

"Yes, for a while. How long, of course, I don't know. Repeatedly I noticed that the common people observed a certain reserve towards me, the student, that they didn't quite see me as one of them, and that despite all their attachment there was still a residue of shyness in them. That bothers me. Look, our Führer has lived through all this; he had to fight hard economic battles in his youth. That's where his deep insights of the people's need and the ways to remedy it come from. That is what I always admire about him, his complete solidarity with the whole of the people. I want to get to know that. In Germany today, a hard battle is raging for the German people and their salvation. It's like war, Mother, and I'm leaving your home to enlist as a war volunteer. Look at it from this side, Mother, and try to understand my leaving you. I can't help it," he said, moved.

His mother's kind eyes rested on her son's face full of heartfelt love; her gentle hand stroked his thick blond hair.

"No, you can't help it. . . . You have fledged, my young falcon; you no longer belong to me alone, but to all of them, to the comrades of the SA, to the whole German people. Go with God!" she whispered.

A warm feeling of happiness welled up in Horst. To know that his beloved mother understood him and his actions and judged him fairly was an uplifting thought. And he would need it, because it was not easy to endure such a change of life from the secure son of a middle-class man to a wage-earning worker. But Horst Wessel managed it.

So he became a taxi driver, whizzed through the traffic-ridden streets of Berlin on day or night duty and lived in his simple apartment, detached from everything, no longer a student but a worker. Now he stood in the middle of the people. He was in direct contact with the working classes. When he had to wait at the bus stops with his fellow workers, he saw it as a good opportunity to promote the good cause. He found all types and shades, but most of the taxi drivers belonged to the SPD or the KPD.[30] He campaigned tirelessly, and often with success.

---

[30] The Social Democratic Party and the Communist Party.

But he soon felt that this was not the right profession. Sitting in a car like that, dashing around the streets of Berlin, then again chatting for hours at the car parks with his workmates: that was not the right "work" in his opinion. So he became a shovelman on the underground railway, working with shovel and pickaxe in the sweat of his brow among the many others from morning until night. Only now was he in the middle of it all.

It wasn't easy for him. It was a completely different kind of activity, like sport. How exhausted he felt when he returned home in the evening. Every muscle in his body ached, and sometimes the thought arose in this physical fatigue: *why don't you return to the house on the Jüdenstraße?* But he remained firm. The next morning he was back at work, shoveling and chopping as if he had never done anything else in his life. He chewed his way through painful days until his hands were calloused and chunky: real manual laborer's fists.

Rumors about him circulated during this time. It was said that the Nazi student had fallen out with his relatives, and was no longer getting money to study because he was taking part in the Nazi racket, and was now forced to earn his bread as a laborer.

His comrades knew better. But they remained silent, looking with respectful glances at his battered hands, and Horst felt as if they were now squeezing his hand much tighter and more firmly when they shook hands. He felt that he had come even closer to these people, with whom he had now been fighting shoulder-to-shoulder for so long, by entering their world. And it made him happy.

If at all possible, he would have his Storm 5 line up at the Jüdenhof in the evenings. There was often enough opportunity to pay a short visit to his mother's apartment. He never gave up contact with his loved ones at home. It even happened that he came home late in the evening or in the middle of the night. As usual, he sat down at his mother's bedside and told her about the things that troubled and excited his mind. At various times he asked for money and received it; but he did not spend the contributions on himself, but sacrificed them for his storm or for the movement.

During this period there was also an episode of cheerfulness, which, however, is quite characteristic of the young *Sturmführer*'s quick-tempered manner.

One evening he returned home earlier than usual and said merrily, "there's nothing more for me to do today—this evening I am yours!"

His sister Inge was already ready to go out in a festive evening dress. Hellmut Mingard, a young doctor and friend of the Wessel family, was also present. When Horst asked him, he found out that they were going to a dance at the *Korpshaus* in Grunewald. They asked him to join them.

He didn't really like that, but when his mother talked him into it, he agreed. First, of course, he had to wash and clean himself thoroughly before he could dress in the clothes prescribed for such events. Black suit, silk socks, and pleated dress shirt are unknown items in the world of the shipper.

He was just busy knotting his neck tie when a violent noise penetrated the silence of his room. The front door slammed, thudding footsteps sounded on the stairs, and loud voices announced that something was disturbing the peace.

But then his brother Werner rushed into Horst's room and breathlessly reported that he and his comrade Erich Ponke, who was in the SA with him in the same storm, had been attacked by a pack of Red Front members in the immediate vicinity of the house. They had only been able to save themselves with difficulty, but his comrade's bicycle had remained in the hands of the attackers.

"Did you recognize the scoundrels?" asked Horst.

"It seemed to me that we were dealing with the *Schlageter* clique," said Werner.

"No chance," interjected comrade Ponke, who had joined them. "They were from the gang of the *Siebenhaar*. I recognized the guy myself!"

So, the holster was put on, and Horst quickly grabbed his pistol, dashed down the stairs and ran along the street the next minute before those following him quite grasped what was happening. Mingard, who didn't even know what was going on, also snatched a stick from the stand and chased after the trio.

"Heavenly Father, how may this end! The boy is racing like a madman towards the sinister crowd," said the worried mother, who had hurried to the window with her daughter. But suddenly she turned to Inge and said reproachfully, "I don't understand how you can still laugh at that!"

"But mother, dear! It's hilarious how Horst looks; I can't help but laugh," Inge replied.

It was indeed a sight to laugh at. Without shoes, in bare stockings, a tailcoat shirt, and with a fluttering tie, holding his strapless trousers with his left hand while his right hand clutched his gun: that's how Horst raced along the empty alley—after the enemies.

But he did not feel ridiculous at all. The student from the Jüdenstraße had the reputation of being a ruthless, hard-hitting fighter. And even though he came in his stockings, the reds thought it best to put on their stockings as well. So they bolted and abandoned the captured bicycle—only to get away from the proximity of this dreaded *Sturmführer* 5.

Horst picked up the bike, but then the trousers fell off completely. Laughing, his friends followed and made sure that Horst's hands were free to hold on to his trousers for the time being. Then they went home, where Inge cheerfully congratulated her brother on his heroic deed, but advised him not to forget his suspenders the next time he went out to do chivalrous deeds.

Since Horst now had to clean his dusty trousers again, which took some time, mother and sister went ahead with Mingard to the *Korpshaus*, with Horst to follow.

While he was brushing his trousers, he asked his brother, "Well, how about you, Werner? Are you coming?"

"No—I'm on duty tonight," he replied, "meeting at the Märchenbrunnen in Friedrichshain. It's a messy affair, because the reds are going to try to blow things up. Of course, no man in the storm should be absent."

Horst listened. This was going to be fun. He had already heard something about it. With one leap he was at the telephone, called the *Korpshaus*, and asked that his mother be told that something important was preventing him from coming after her, and that she would excuse him. He tore off his white shirt and got back into his work clothes. After quickly asking his brother to tell him where the storm was meeting, he set off.

In a short time he managed to round up sixteen of his men. The small crowd was greeted joyfully by the storm of Barrikadenalbert, of which Werner Wessel was a member.

"Hello, you're just in time! It's going to be a rowdy affair tonight," Sprengel called out to them.

Then they marched off. This time it was a march with obstacles. Not only Red Front members occupied the streets, but also Reichsbanner detachments had joined them. There was constant skirmishing, sometimes at the front, sometimes in the middle, then again at the end of the marching column. But they fought their way through and left the enemy with nothing to show for it.

Horst saw immediately when he looked over the packed hall that it was two-thirds full of opponents. It would make for a great show today. He saw it coming. You could hear in the muffled roar of voices that the air was full of tension, which was bound to erupt into a wild hall battle any minute.

Horst quickly agreed with Sprengel on the distribution of the people. They only had about eighty men to face this enormous crowd. But that did not make them discouraged.

Right from the start, they had a firm grip and every troublemaker was brought out into the fresh air with ruthless severity. And so they succeeded in making the speakers heard.

After about ten minutes a thunderous bang interrupted the speaker and clouds of smoke and soot darkened the hall. The communists had placed an explosive device, a cannon shell, in the mighty furnace. The force of the explosion tore the old stove to pieces.

That was the signal. The mob howled. "SA out! SA out!" roared the wild chorus.

But the small crowd was not afraid. In an instant the leaders had made themselves understood. Barrikadenalbert and his men occupied the main entrance, while Horst and the others let the reds and Nazis out in a wild confusion. In vain the reds stormed against Sprengel and his troops in order to break through, but they had to retreat again and again with their heads covered in blood.

Finally the hall was cleared. But now came the worst: they had to fight their way through a raging, wild wave of people in order to get out themselves.

"Get out of here, Albert, or the communists will attack us through the doors from the side!" shouted Horst to Sprengel.

"Don't any of you have a gun?" he asked back.

"Nah—no can do, the orders from *OSAF* are that no firearms are to be taken along."

"Damn it! They were up in arms when the order came out. But it doesn't help—go for the enemy—he shall now get to know our fists!" exclaimed Barrikadenalbert angrily.

Closed in rows of four, they burst out through the outward-facing door. A howling wave of people, roaring with hatred, piled up around the entrance. As always, it retreated before the first fierce impact of those bravely attacking with their bare fists. The *Schupo* men covered their backs; they had breathing room.

But then, once the weak squad had been divided into the blindly striking crowd, it became dangerous. A break-up of the column would have meant the end. But Horst Wessel's eye was on them; he made sure that they stayed in contact. He had to defend himself as well as the last SA man. Yes, most of them had it in for him. In their eyes he was their greatest pest.

Forward they went in dense rows. Everyone knew that breaking away meant certain death. Sprengel, Fiedler, and the Wessel brothers marched in the front line. They already knew what was at stake. When they arrived at Straußberger Platz, a hail of stones pelted them from the front.

In the wild shouting of the frenzied crowd, there was only the faint sound of the provocative clatter of the Mauser pistols with which the *Schupo* men at the end of the procession made themselves heard.

But soon the shooting died away behind them. They were alone in the face of the masses that had sworn their doom.

But they were dealing with a determined and united force that knew all the practices of street fighting and was excellently led. The eyes of the leaders in this furious battle that raged through the dark streets of Berlin spotted every opportunity that presented itself, dodging the enemy here and dashing through a gap into a less crowded side street there. Always forward, always with a firm marching step, crisscrossing the streets until they reached some railway station, from where they went home—individually and in small squads.

Jannowitzbrücke station was the next destination, but it was surrounded by a roaring crowd. They were met by a howling, polyphonic chorus of angry invectives and threats. "Death to the fascist dogs! Throw them into the Spree!"

"Forward! We must get through! I'm sick of marching around!" shouted Horst Wessel to the friendly *Sturmführer*.

"I've been sick of it for a long time, too. Get on with it!" was Sprengel's reply.

With grim defiance, the Brownshirts threw themselves against the raging crowd, breaking with a powerful impact into the wall of people salivating with hatred. The fight lasted less than half an hour. By then the brave SA troops had fought their way through. And not one man was lost in the whirling back and forth of the struggle.

Seventeen seriously wounded were counted among the numerous injured. They drove around all over Berlin, and soon at this station, soon at that, a small group got off to go home or to accommodate a seriously wounded person.

The whole of red Berlin seemed to be arrayed against the small group of the SA, and yet not a single man was missing, a proof of the strength of the people and the efficiency of the leaders.

Werner Wessel had also been hit. Horst took him home. First he listened to see if his mother was back yet. She had not yet returned home.

"Quick, Werner, wash yourself! Your face is full of blood, and the laundry has to be cleaned so that tomorrow Mother won't find any trace of the fight," Horst said to the brother.

"You'll stay here, won't you, Horst?" said the brother.

"No can do. I have to get up early again tomorrow morning and go to work. Sleep well, boy, after a lively evening," was the answer. Nodding once more to his brother, he left the room.

Horst Wessel wandered home through the streets of nocturnal Berlin to his poor shack. Instead of spending the evening in good clothes and cheerful company with musical recitals and dancing in a quiet, hospitable place, he had struggled with the lowest class of the people and bravely risked his life for the victory of his Führer's great ideal for the liberation of Germany.

Warned Again

Horst Wessel comes home from work tired as a dog. A letter lies on the table. He tears open the envelope and skims over the few lines scrawled in pencil on the note:

"Dear Mr. W.! Come to the Magazinstraße today after eleven. It's about Nazitod."[31]

Hmm—a highly suspicious thing. The writing makes a childishly clumsy impression. Who might have written it? And they want to meet in the quiet street, a little away from the main stream of traffic?

---

[31] Nazi-Death.

At least it's not so dangerous there. The term *Nazitod* makes one think. The reds don't have such an excellent structure as the SA, where the individual cliques were usually given the name or nickname of their leader. The gang Nazitod was quite a rough company and was not inferior to the wild gang of the Schlageter.

After all, it could be a nasty trap, but he would go there anyway. Of course, with all due caution.

Several times he had been walking back and forth in the Magazinstraße at the appointed time when he suddenly heard light footsteps behind him. He turned around immediately. A girl was coming towards him.

"Did you summon me here?" he asked.

"Yes, it's about the Nazitod," she admitted.

"Ah—I know you—aren't you—"

"Erna, yes," she helped him remember.

That was the girl he had freed from the hands of the brute and to whom he had given the travel money his grandmother had given him.

"So, what's going on?" he asked curiously.

Hastily the sentences came out of the girl's mouth. She warned him urgently. The red camp was determined to get rid of the "Terror of the East." They were waiting for him everywhere, because he went out alone so much. Everything had been spied out: which meetings he attended, when he went home, and where he went on certain days. There was a spy network around him, she said, and for God's sake he should be careful.

This interested him, but in the certain expectation of learning more and more definite details about the enemy's plans, he invited her for a glass of beer and went with her to a pub where he questioned her.

He further learned that the red group Schlageter had actually received the order to bust him, but since the members of Schlageter had been arrested themselves in the meantime, the gang Nazitod had taken over the execution of the order. When Horst asked who had given the order for the surveillance on him, the girl explained that she didn't know exactly, but since all the clique bosses (that was the name of the leaders of the red groups) went in and out of the Lieb-knechthaus, it could be assumed that the order had come from there.

"Do you know what they plan to do to me? A good thrashing, of course, and I'll be lucky if I get six months in the hospital out of it," he asked with a laugh.

She nodded affirmatively and answered his further questions about the conditions and measures in the red camp with great frankness. He learned that she herself had observed him on behalf of the communists, found out where he lived, and investigated his habits. She had passed on the information about where he lived truthfully, since this would have been found out soon enough, but she would passed on all other information falsely and distortedly.

"So, you lied to your red employer! Do you also know, girl, what will happen to you if this comes out? Then you'll be in bad trouble. Why did you do it?" he asked.

She was silent, then she looked at him gratefully with her good, faithful eyes and said, "I did it for you, because back then, when I was in such a bad place, you gave me all that money in Mexico. No one has ever been so good to me."

The mistrust Horst felt at first faded away, the way this simple girl from the crowd spoke to him like that. No, those good eyes could not lie. Erna was no traitor, but an honest, grateful creature.

But her more personal qualities immediately took a back seat to the great goal for which he was working. He saw an opportunity here to get accurate news from the enemy camp and asked Erna if she wanted to work for the National Socialists.

She immediately agreed and declared that she would do everything he asked of her; that she would be faithful. That was an important thing for Horst. But it did not escape him that Erna looked tired and weary. His human compassion for the community member awoke. When, on questioning, she admitted that she hadn't eaten anything yet, he immediately ordered her a hearty meal. While she ate, she told him that the landlady had stolen some of the money she had been given, but that she still had some left and hoped that her sewing would soon improve and that she would be able to earn enough to live on.

Wessel was glad that Camillo Roß had been wrong with his mocking remark about the useless money he had given away. There was no doubt that the girl had remained good and was seriously trying to get by honestly. When he found out that she was without a permanent home since the landlady had stolen from her, he took her away and brought her to his own landlady, Frau Salm, that treacherous widow of a communist who played such a fatal part in the attack in which Horst received his fatal wound.

With a rare loyalty this common girl served Horst Wessel and his cause. She looked after the simple worker, washed his work clothes, kept them in order, and cared for him in an emotion of inextinguishable gratitude. At the same time, however, she did scouting duty for the SA in the red camp: an extremely dangerous task, which she carried out with the simple bravery that characterized her whole being.

No one else knew about this except Horst Wessel, and his respect and gratitude for this sacrifice were great. When his comrades, Sprengel and Fiedler, once did not speak of her with the respect he thought was due her, he reprimanded them and told them that he would become engaged to this faithful girl. From then on, they all treated the quiet Erna with the greatest respect. In this, too, the German Horst Wessel showed his attachment to the people. He had the opportunity to look for a wife from the wealthy classes of life, but he chose a child from the people. But a violent death destroyed this hope as well.

There was a beautiful bond of blood and existence in the circles of the SA and all those who were close to the comrades. How much this was the case and how helpful Horst Wessel was to the relatives of his comrades is best demonstrated by one incident. One Saturday Horst came home from work with his salary. A poor, pale woman was waiting for him: it was the bride of his comrade Ewald, who had been arrested for beating up a few reds too hard. She was in distress, looked at him with tear-stained eyes, and he gave her the money bag with all its contents, forcing it on her when she only wanted to take a part. For this he had slaved for a whole week.

No wonder they all clung to him with all the unbroken love of German working men, adored him and followed him everywhere with courage and enthusiasm. It was also he who brought to life the willingness of his fellow workers to make sacrifices. The money they earned through overtime was given to their unemployed comrades.

He was tirelessly active in his struggles to win over the German soul for the ideal of liberation. One day at the workplace the subject of unemployment stamps came up, and the circumstances surrounding it were described. Horst Wessel, a former student and now a shipper, had never had the opportunity to stamp. When he found out that the communists wanted to do the talking and pull the stamp brothers over to them with harsh terror, his spirit of action sprang up.

What, the communists saw the squares in front of the stamp offices as their very own advertising area for members? There could be no such thing! Out of the question! To drive them away from there was to be a matter of honor from then on. He was so preoccupied with the thought of this defensive struggle that he did not even take time to change his working clothes, but after finishing his work ran to the *Staf* standing at the door and discussed with him the defense and advertising plans for the squares and rooms around the stamp offices.

Now the communists were also attacked in those places which had hitherto been considered their undisputed territory, and there they were broken with all their might. And again it was the work of Horst Wessel that the enemies felt here, the German youth in whose soul the great longing for the freedom of his people was alive.

During the November days of 1929, things were extremely lively, as they always were in the times before the election. The Berlin SA was always fighting with someone, sometimes with the Red Front, sometimes with the Reichsbanner, and sometimes with the *Schupo* men. Injuries occurred daily. There were also deaths, and the injured had long since ceased to be counted in the reports.

Once, when the comrades were driving back from the Weißensee by train at night, Horst Wessel received the order from *Staf* 4 to write the report. He was ready immediately, but took the piece of paper, on which some preparatory notes were written, with his left hand. His right arm had been hit with an iron bar that day. They walked together through the notorious Fischerkietz, which was a communist stronghold, and went to the Bombenschloß, where the SA comrade Richard Fiedler lived, Petristraße 15. The name for the ancient house, which was in the middle of the Bolshevik quarter, had been given to it by the Red Front. The numerous bullet holes in the carved gate testified to fierce battles that had raged around the Bombenschloß.

First Horst Wessel's injuries were examined, and after it was established with satisfaction that the bone was intact, it was bandaged. Of course, this was not entirely painless, and Horst pulled out his cigarette box to smoke a little while they were doing it. With the tin, he pulled out a small cardboard card.

"Well, who put this in my pocket? A recommendation card from the Red Front? Someone must have slipped it into my pocket when we were hanging out on the Parkstraße," Horst said.

"I'm sure they did," agreed Gerhard Pantel. "Usually they are masters at emptying pockets, but this time they did it the other way round. Let's hear what they have to write to you."

Horst read aloud, "Ludwig Horst Wessel, beware! Death to you and all fascist dogs!"

"The order of the names is wrong. It should be 'Horst Ludwig,'" said Werner Wessel, who was also there.

Fiedler took the note with the mean threat, which also contained an expletive, and angrily pocketed it. Horst himself paid no further attention to the death notice. He knew that he was on the blacklist of his opponents and that they wanted to kill him in their evil lust for murder, so he did not get upset because of such a note. Conscious of his faithful fulfillment of duty to the people and the Fatherland as a champion of Adolf Hitler's National Socialism, he continued unflinchingly along the path prescribed by his thirst for action.

Election Sunday! A sea of flags waved in the streets of Berlin. The red of the Social Democrats and the red of the Communists with the Soviet sign of the sickle and hammer predominated, only occasionally and almost timidly did the black-red-yellow banner of the Weimar Republic show itself.

Trucks thundered through the streets, manned by Brownshirts, above whose heads the red swastika banner fluttered in the November wind as the herald of the German freedom and uprising movement.

The brown fighters saw it as a point of honor that they should drive through the worst communist quarters first. In vain, the leaders of the accompanying police cars pleaded with them to avoid the wildest areas and not to provoke the agitated opponents even more. Nothing could be done, though, so they drove off. They drove right into the seething, boiling cauldron of the red districts, where they were met by a wild crowd roaring and raging.

So they came to Wedding, where the crowds were gathering. A hail of stones pelted down on the cars like a thunderstorm. The crowd surrounded them like a surging, boiling sea. The cars were caught in the middle. It was dangerous, for if the onrushing wave of people foamed up and swept them down, all was lost.

An unbridled will to destroy sparkled in the eyes of the onrushing people and spoke clearly from their rage-distorted expressions.

Horst Wessel handed the flag to a comrade and pushed his way to the front of the wagon.

"Fire away, man—it's high time!" he shouted to the driver. The driver just nodded. He had understood, pulled the key out of the switch box, and backfires started like cannon blasts, drowning out the booming howls. That helped. Horrified, the basically cowardly crowd recoiled, thinking that they were being fired upon, and then there was some quiet. This time it had gone well.

The journey continued. The swastika banner was to be carried through the whole of Berlin on this day. In Tegel, the cars were stopped by swarming *Schupo* men. "Pull over for a weapons-check!" In the Kösliner Straße, Nazis were said to have fired on harmless workers. Such rumors were always spread on the orders of the opponents and readily believed by the police.

In the guardroom they even had to undress, oh—for the umpteenth time on this memorable day! This did not embitter them, no, it only stimulated their sense of humor and was taken lightly.

A squad leader in Horst Wessel's storm, Ernst Schulz, was full of fresh humor. He stood at attention in front of the examining officer and reported, "I have a hollow tooth, Officer, don't you want to take a look inside? Maybe there's a machine gun in it." He opened his mouth wide and stuck out his tongue.

Well, the officers laughed, but it didn't help. They were all arrested, and the whole standard was led to the Alex. They didn't sing on the way there, but they whistled the *"Seeräuberlied,"* a mockery of Police Chief Weiß.

Der mächtigste König von Groß-Berlin
Das ist der Isidor Weiß.
Doch Doktor Goebbels, der Oberbandit,
Der macht ihm die Hölle heiß.

The most powerful king of Greater Berlin
That is Isidor Weiß.
But Dr. Goebbels, the chief bandit,
Makes hell hot for him.

The policemen knew the words and perhaps hummed it along with the whistles, but the name "Isidor," which in Berlin at that time was considered the worst insult to his majesty and was punishable, was not spoken, only whistled.[32]

But as the numerous police cars surrounded the procession of National Socialists and accompanied it to Alexanderplatz, the SA's chant of protection resounded through the streets, roaring and carried by enthusiasm: *"Die Fahnen hoch! Die Reihen dicht geschlossen!"*[33]

And then, as they marched in an orderly procession from the Magazinstraße to the police headquarters, a chorus thundered accusingly: *"Weil die Kommunisten morden, Sind wir verhaftet worden."*[34]

The entire standard was housed in a prison with the derisive name "Alter Hundestall."[35] Everyone was to be questioned individually: a most tedious affair. The officials begged and admonished, but, good heavens, when a few hundred young, eager men are together, it is not as quiet as it is in a girls' school. They became mischievous and played all kinds of games, which the police officers did well not to notice, for they would only have been annoyed by them.

Werner Wessel squatted in a corner and wrote busily. When he finished, he jumped onto the bench, waved the sheet of paper and shouted into the crowd, "Quiet! A new, beautiful poem is done! Have you ever heard of the 'Nasobēm'?"

"Come on—what kind of a thing is that!" echoed back to him.

"A very strange creature with a powerful nose; it comes from a poem by the old Morgenstern. You know him, I've often read you the funny verses he wrote. And now I'm going to read you something that I've adapted for the SA here in the 'Old Dog House.' Pay attention!"

---

[32] Here, "Isidor" refers to Berhard Weiß, a Jewish lawyer and police chief in Berlin during the time of the Weimar Republic. He was opposed to National Socialism and banned the Berlin branch of the NSDAP in 1927. As a result, Joseph Goebbels, then *Gauleiter* in Berlin, gave him the nickname Isidor—a name which at that time was commonly held by Jews—in his newspaper *Der Angriff*. Goebbels chose this name to suggest that Bernhard had Germanized his first name. Weiß would go on to successfully sue Goebbels on multiple occasions, although Goebbels did not let it bother him. Weiß was fired from his position in 1932 and fled to England right before Adolf Hitler became Chancellor.
[33] "Raise the flags! The ranks tightly closed!
[34] "Because the communists are killing, we've been arrested."
[35] Old Dog House.

Auf krummen Beinen schreitet
Einher das Nasobem,
Von Schupos rings begleitet,
Hübsch sicher und bequem.

Es schleicht am Alexander
Aus seinem Bau hervor,
Erschröcklich wie ein Panther —
Man ruft es Isidor.

Das mag es gar nicht haben;
Wut speit es, Dreck und Lehm!
Drum nennen's brave Knaben
Auch nur das Nasobem!

On crooked legs
The nasobem strides along,
Accompanied by Shupo's all around,
Handsomely and comfortably for sure.

It creeps out of its den
At Alexanderplatz,
Frightened like a panther—
It is called Isidor.

It doesn't like that at all;
It spits rage, dirt and clay!
That's why good boys
Call it the Nasobem!

Cheering applause roared through the room after the reading of this new mocking poem about the Jewish police chief of the time. The detectives emphatically restored calm, but they did so with an undisguised smirk; they could take a joke too, the bourgeois. And one of them asked for a copy—not officially of course.

Staf and *Sturmführer* had finally made the upper officials understand that mass-arrest was a quite senseless measure, and so the people were gradually released in small groups. Always in groups of three or four, so that the Red Front, which was on night patrol en masse, could lie in wait for them and take it easy on them.

Thus ended the memorable election campaign in November 1929.

Dark Days Are Dawning

A bond of warm love and mutual understanding embraced the four people in the apartment in the Jüdenstraße. As much as Horst Wessel's whole being was gripped and taken up by his activity in the SA and in the movement for the spread of National Socialism in Germany, his strong courageous heart also had a wealth of love to share with those closest to him. It could not be otherwise. Despite all the holy urge for the high patriotic goals he was striving for, he could never fall into ruthlessness and neglect his relatives for the sake of the whole.

In his brother Werner he also saw the brave SA comrade and was pleased when he wanted to emulate him in many things. He praised his Christmas plays and songs, which he wrote for his Storm 1, and so the same urge to be active in the national movement deepened the brotherly feelings that both brothers had for each other. As capable as the younger brother was, he did not possess the mental willpower and, above all, the outstanding leadership qualities of the elder Horst.

Inge, their dear little sister with a fresh sense of humor, had grown very fond of Horst. Because of her straight, purposeful character and the liveliness of her vibrant nature, he held her in high esteem and highly valued her hard work.

However, Horst's relationship with his mother was particularly close. There was a beautiful communion between them in thinking, feeling, and understanding. Horst Wessel had already been a *Sturmführer* for a long time, had already done many a manly deed that earned him the highest recognition, but to his mother he remained the child, the boy, who revealed all the stirrings of his soul and all the thoughts that weighed him down or moved him to his mother in faithful trust.

This faithful mother embraced all three children with the same love. But for Horst her feeling was stronger for the reason that he, in his courageous use of his personality, without regard for the dangers involved, caused her by far the greater concern.

The rare unity that prevailed in this family comes across quite clearly when considering the time that Horst left his parents' home. He left his loved ones to become a worker, descended into another, lower class, but nothing, nothing at all changed in the feelings of those left behind for him, who had put on the simple worker's garment and really became a worker. They remained as before, they associated with him as before, perhaps they even respected him a little more for the sake of his courageous convincing deed. In this community, from which Horst Wessel was given to the German people and especially to the German youth, harmonious, mutual love and unconditional trust prevailed, as they are exemplary for German family life.

Christmas was near. The scent of fir trees was already wafting through the house. Werner had bought the tree. Then an urgent letter brought trouble. Two of his mother's brothers had been living in South America for decades—one in Argentina, the other in Chile. It had always been a secret wish of hers to give her two sons the opportunity to visit their relatives. She knew how much her boys would like to get to know foreign countries first-hand. A ship's captain, an old friend of her late husband, had agreed to take one of the brothers along free of charge and bring him back again. Since everything was in order and ready, and with the ship sailing in two days, Werner had to travel immediately.

Horst had already refused earlier. He could not abandon work now at such an eventful time, he explained.

When the letter arrived, Horst was not at home. He was staying at his place of work. Werner and Inge delved into the maps to follow the journey in its various stages. The younger brother was quite enthusiastic about the whole thing, but it seemed to him that he was being favored over his older brother. That thought did not allow him to rest and enjoy the anticipation undisturbed. He called Horst on the phone and told the astonished listener quite selflessly that he would gladly forego the trip if Horst wanted to make use of the advantageous offer.

"That's really nice of you, little brother, but I can't leave my Storm 5 now; I'm indispensable here. You know yourself that serious times are ahead and every man must be at his post," was the reply.

The hint gripped Werner. He had forgotten in the surging joy that hard battles were on their way. His mother saw the extinguishing of the warm joy in her boy's face. She suspected what was going on, picked up the phone herself, and discuss the case with Horst.

"Well, what does Horst think, Mother?" asked Werner as she put the receiver down on the fork.

"He says that he can't give you any advice in this matter; everyone has to know for himself what duty demands of him," the mother replied.

"Then I, too, will renounce and hold out in Storm 1 at my post in the SA," the young man declared, completely filled with his brother's sense of sacrifice and loyalty.

His mother and his sister Inge tried to change his mind by pointing out to him that a similar opportunity to visit foreign countries would never present itself again. But Werner remained firm; his brother's word of duty had hooked into his conscience, and so he forewent all of the glorious pleasures of such a journey. For the Wessel brothers, willingness to sacrifice was a self-evident duty.

Another, albeit much more modest, pleasure was in store for Werner: a ski trip lasting several days in the wintry snowfields of the Giant Mountains. He had also asked Horst for his advice on this. Two opportunities presented themselves for him to join in. The old comrades from the scout association, tried and tested skiers, wanted him to join them, but so did a Nazi skiing group, which, however, could not match the sporting achievements of his old comrades.

"What do you think, which should I join?" asked Werner of his brother. "The friends from our group make a point of me coming along; some of them I know very well."

Horst replied, "Well, join them then; they need a rest after the strenuous service of the last few weeks. Your scout friends can do without you for once. God be with you, dear boy, and greet the white winter splendor in the mountains for me."

Werner faithfully followed his brother's advice and joined the group of young National Socialists. Eighteen youths, a few girls among them, drove to Hirschberg one Saturday evening, where they first fulfilled their civic duty by registering on the list of the people's petition against the Young Plan, and then threw themselves into the sport with all the energy of youth and the desire of their young hearts. The white, sunlit snow fields attracted them.

But invisibly the hand of fate wove its threads. Not everyone returned from this journey into the snowy mountains; some— including Werner Wessel—were trapped by the snow in its cold bed, where they sank into a sleep from which there was no awakening.

Werner Wessel fought with all of the courage of a young man trained in battle, but the forces of the storm were stronger than his hot will. Having reached the end of his strength, he sank into a deep snowdrift and fell asleep, his eyes closed, never to see the dawn of German Liberation-Day!

The four victims of the cold ice giants lay were laid out in the simple little church of Wang in Krummhübel: Hans Tesche from nearby Hirschberg, Werner Wessel, Fritz Radloff, and Hildegard, a young girl.

Horst had travelled to Silesia with his mother and Aunt Gerti on hearing the terrible news, and now they stood before the victims laid out on scented pine greenery, their rosy, freshly colored faces not reminding the onlookers of death and separation.

A sob escaped from the mother's lips when she saw her boy lying so still. It was so hard for her to believe that he was gone from her forever. She kissed him once more, then staggered out and drove back to Berlin with her sister.

Horst had promised his mother to bring the beloved dead man home as soon as possible. But when he set about carrying out his plan, he was faced with immense difficulties. The regulations governing the transport of corpses by rail required the completion of a vast amount of formalities. And his mother was waiting.

Horst's patience had run out, so he drove to Berlin, looked for a car, took a reliable driver from his Storm 5 with him, and arrived back at the little church of Wang after a twelve-hour drive. Comrades from the Hirschberg SA helped to put the dead comrades and the girl into the coffins brought from Berlin, and the saddest journey in Horst Wessel's life through the snow-covered countryside and on icy country roads began.

He had been driving for hours, not letting his comrade take the wheel, because he wanted to drive his dear brother home himself. Oh, now he felt with all his soul how much he had loved the bright-eyed boy.

It was not only the physical exertions and the lack of food and rest that were hard on him; much worse was the hard pressure of the reproaches he felt because he had advised his brother to join the less-experienced Nazi skiing group. This thought that he might be to blame because his brother had perished in the snowstorm tormented the sensitive Horst Wessel terribly. So he fell into brooding, painful brooding. "If only I had persuaded him to make the journey to America, he would now be on the steamship and alive!"

And if he then told himself that in the given case he would do the same again, it was a weak, not long-lasting consolation. His peace was gone, a worm gnawed inside him, and dark shadows dampened all joy and zest for life in the days that were still granted to him by fate. Ah, there were only a few of them left.

The people from Storm 1 experienced a deep pain: their best had passed away. A dull pressure weighed on them. They faithfully kept the wake after laying out the young fighter, who lay still and rigid.

And the hour dawned when they had to take the coffin on their shoulders to carry it down. The bright words of command, "SA, halt! Eyes to the left!" tore the restrained silence. Swastika flags were lowered in front of the dead comrade. The drums rattled muffled, the music played, the procession set off in the falling dusk, doused in gloomy, blazing torchlight.

A final farewell! Dr. Goebbels had rushed from the Rhineland to pay his last respects to his comrade. *Staf* 4 found moving words at the grave of the loyal storm trooper of Standard 4. The final chorus, muffled and solemn, echoed over the crowd of thousands that filled the vast Nikolai cemetery:

> *Du kleiner Tambour, schlag ein,*
> *Kameraden, laßt die Banner wehen,*
> *Wir wolln nicht länger Knechte sein,*
> *Alldeutschland sieht ein Auferstehen!*
> *Lebe wohl, leb wohl, du stolze Zier,*
> *Du Sturmsoldat von der Standarte vier!*

> You little drummer, play a tune,
> Comrades, let the banners wave,
> We no longer want to be slaves
> All of Germany will rise again!
> Farewell, farewell, you proud jewel,
> You Stormtrooper of Standard 4!

His song, Werner Wessel's song, they sang into the open tomb with the deepest feeling of which German comrades are capable. The mother's pain was stark. With great sorrow, Dr. Goebbels realized that she was denied the benefit of soothing tears.

The gathering of mourners dispersed. The cemetery emptied. Only one, a single one stood at the fresh grave—Horst Wessel. All alone he took leave of his dead brother who took a piece of his heart with him into his silent, cool grave, and left the unsatisfied love in a pain-stricken, shaken brother's heart.

Sickness and Murderous Thugs Attack Horst Wessel

With all the genuine love of simple working-class people, the comrades of the SA and their relatives clung to *Sturmführer* 5. Thus the mother of Barrikadenalbert had also taken the young student into her heart. Albert Sprengel had been dismissed as Truppführer because of his rebellious spirit and was now back on duty as a simple SA man.

Tired, he came home from duty one evening. While he ate what his mother prepared for him, the simple woman told him about Horst Wessel, about whom she was very worried.

"I tell you, Albert, it was too much what had befallen the good boy in the last few days," the good woman complained. "He was all confused the other day when he came here to discuss something with you. You can count on it, he'll collapse now that his brother's funeral is over, and the tension that keeps him going will fade. He looked very miserable; there's a sickness in him."

"I've been worried about his poor appearance too, Mother," Sprengel agreed.

"He must get away from the Frankfurter Straße and go back home to mother!" declared Mrs. Sprengel. "There is no substitute for maternal care. He is most likely to recover under the eyes of his mother and sister."

"Hmm, that's quite good, but it won't be an easy matter to get him to make the move. He has now got it into his head to live like one of our own. 'I don't want to be better off than my comrades,' he says briefly, if anyone utters a word about it. He has a hard head about it," sighed Sprengel.

"But he will obey if the *Staf* or the *Gauleiter*, Dr. Goebbels, orders him to leave the old shack and move back to his mother's house on the Jüdenstraße," said the good old lady.

"I want to talk to my comrades about it," said Albert.

"You do that. Horst Wessel has to go into proper care as soon as possible; he's sicker than he seems. Good Erna is not capable of taking care of him alone," his mother explained.

Albert Sprengel went to Fiedler's Bombenschloß. The Christmas tree was alight there, but the mood was gloomy. Barrikadenalbert growled something about "spoiled Christmas," wanted to "throw the tree out the window," and Fiedler was also in a gloomy mood. The death of their young, sunny and cheerful comrade Werner Wessel weighed heavily on them.

Then the telephone rang. It was Erna calling them. The two of them immediately set out for her and met her at the agreed street corner.

"They've done away with Roß," she reported shyly.

"Ah—Camillo Roß, the Red Front member! What happened? Who was there? Is he completely finished off—or just wounded?" urged Fiedler.

Erna didn't know anything for sure. The communists assumed that it was SA who had fatally wounded Roß. But one thing was certain: they would take revenge, Erna claimed. She had been asking around everywhere and had noticed increased activity in the red camp. But everything was handled so secretly that nothing went beyond a narrow circle. She was also suspicious of the widow Salm's industriousness, running from one red bar to the next. She—Erna— feared that something was at work against Horst. He didn't want to listen to any warnings and was ill—seriously ill; he was only keeping himself upright with all his efforts. The best thing would be if he could be taken away from the dangerous surroundings and moved to the Jüdenstraße, because he would not be safe in the Frankfurter Straße for a moment.

In her heartache, the worried girl poured out her woes to the two SA men.

"Stop it! He has to go!" said Fiedler. "Your mother is right, Albert, and Erna said so, too. It's almost a miracle that the communists haven't attacked him here yet."

"We must get him to the Jüdenstraße, whatever the cost!" decided Sprengel. "After all, in his present condition he is defenseless if they attack him. If necessary, we'll call the police or Dr. Goebbels—he'll have to obey them. Come on, Richard, let's try our luck!"

Against all expectations, they succeeded. Their hearts ached when they noticed Horst's physical weakness, standing before them weak and miserable, looking at them with feverish eyes. He himself felt that his comrades were giving him the best advice when they asked him to go with them to the Jüdenstraße to be healed there. Obediently he followed them into the car and was soon at home in his old room. Motherly love surrounded him; motherly hands, soft and good, nursed him. But it was a hard, painful two weeks. Feverish heat made his body weak and limp. But when it subsided, willpower and the thought of his duties in the movement pulled him up again. In the confused speeches generated by fever, he had, after all, been occupied almost exclusively with his Storm 5, fantasizing in-between about the sad end of his beloved brother. The heavy pressure of this event still weighed on his mind.

His kind mother wanted to use the soft mood that set in when the feverish tension left him and great weakness paralyzed his will to inspire him to go on a trip to South America, from which she hoped for his full recovery and invigoration. Smiling dully, he listened to her words when she told him about the beauties and pleasures of such a journey to the glorious south. All was ready for it. He himself dreamed of it and thought of joyful pleasures, like a boy looking forward to a promised toy.

But nothing came of it. As soon as he felt stronger again, he no longer thought of going on a pleasure-trip to South America. Here in Berlin, in the SA, was his place. As his physical strength increased, so did his mental strength, and this showed him his place in the fight for Germany's freedom. There was only one thing his mother had achieved: he wanted to give up the workers' apartment in the Frankfurter Straße and go back to live with his mother in the Jüdenstraße.

He had to go there again, he explained to his mother. She strongly advised him not to. He could send for his things. And if Erna needed something, she would gladly be given it. She suspected that dangers were lurking there for the boy, because the SA comrades wanted so badly for him to not return there.

But Horst Wessel was not persuaded. He went. Like a true hero who never retreats from the enemy, he strode towards his doom. He must have known the treachery of the enemy, but he paid no attention to it in his calm self-evident boldness.

As he strode down the hall, the landlady, Frau Salm, met him. Without returning his greeting, giving him a spiteful look, she slipped into her kitchen, slamming the door behind her. "How that poisonous woman will smile when she finds out that I'm moving out," Horst thought with amusement.

His room was empty and desolate. Erna had probably gone out to do some shopping. He looked around the poor apartment he was about to leave for good. Slowly, he began to pack the things he had brought with him into his suitcase.

Then he paused and began to ponder. How was it going to be? Was he going to leave? To give up this room and return as a fine student to his parents' noble apartment, to bid farewell to the simple life? Wasn't that a cowardly escape? Betrayal of comrades who had it no better? Did he then no longer quite belong to them? Why had he come here? It was only to feel that he belonged to them completely and inseparably.

No, it was not possible; he had to stay! Horst Wessel does not leave his position; he holds out. The ranks are tightly closed! He wrote it himself; this was his place!

Girls' voices disturb him out of deep thought. Erna comes, and Klara, Ewald Bartel's bride, enters the room with her. They greet him joyfully, rejoicing because he looks well and has overcome the illness. Erna's gaze falls on the half-packed suitcase. Immediately she kneels down, wants to help pack. But he fends her off and says firmly, "No; I'm staying!"

The slam of a door startles her.

"Ah, the old serpent, Salm, is leaving. Now we'll have peace for a while," Erna says and adds with a sigh, "she made my life hell while you were away."

Then they sit down together, the three of them, for a cozy chat.

Meanwhile, doom hastens along with the swift steps of the treacherous widow Salm. Her destination is the Bär inn on the Dragonerstraße, the headquarters of the Red Front. Her searching gaze falls on the right fellows for such a cowardly undertaking. The two Jambrowskis, Max Joneck, and a few other Red Front members are there. She sits down with them, tells them that he—Horst Wessel— is at home and urges them not to miss this favorable opportunity. Kupferstein from Warsaw, leader of the red troopers, had ordered that this fascist be eliminated under all circumstances.

They are not willing to do it right away. Horst Wessel is the most feared Nazi fighter, and they have respect for him. Then Else Cohn confronts them: a fanatical anti-fascist girl, she scolds the cowards who are afraid of a boy who is also weakened by a recent illness.

One considers, hesitates. The story is not that simple. What will they tell the police? Well, it is not difficult to make something up. The good Mrs. Salm has just come to get help because she has been mistreated by her lodger, the wild Nazi. Behind such lies, invented with deceitful treachery, the reprehensible vermin wanted to cover themselves when they saved themselves from the downfall that threatened our people from the communist ravagers, who counted Horst Wessel's murderers among their own.

You too, German youth, raise your hands and say a prayer of thanks to the Supreme Guide of the destinies of all peoples and men; for you are free, your blood is pure, and your hearts beat towards a future full of hope.

The Hero's Last Stand

While the evil mob cowardly escapes after the deed is done, the spiteful Frau Salm still dares to search in cupboards and drawers for papers until Erna drives her away. Since Klara is too shaken to call for help, Erna, the brave girl, sets off herself, while Horst Wessel squirms in pain on the floor. Soon help arrives and the poor man is taken to the hospital at Friedrichshain.

The telephone in the house on the Jüdenstraße rings so shrilly. The mother, already tormented by bad premonitions about her son's absence, receives the news of the attack and rushes out into the street, followed by Inge. They drive to the Frankfurter Straße, where they hear from the dismayed but angry SA that Horst has already been taken away, and hurry to the hospital. When they arrive, they see him being carried into the hospital on a swaying stretcher.

Hours of the most bitter agony under the sting of uncertainty come for the two women. The mother's heart clenches as she sees him again, her boy's fresh, proud face is covered by disfiguring bandages, but his eyes—her son's eyes greet her with all the love that lives in him for her. But she is not even allowed to be near him, for the doctors, who have had to operate on the wounded man while he was fully conscious, are adamant in demanding rest for him.

They take him to pavilion seven, where Horst Wessel fights his last heroic battle.

While all over Germany, wherever German hearts beat, a wave of indignation rose over the cowardly deed, the red camp rejoiced and protected the murderers, hiding them and sending them abroad unchallenged. In this way, they confessed to the murderous deed. The threads came together in the Liebknechthaus, where the mastermind was to be found who put the pistol into the fist of the convict Ali Höhler, who fired the fatal shot.

The young hero lay on the bed of pain in pavilion seven, struggling with death for his young life, filled with love for the people and the fight for Germany's freedom, with the bravery that had been praised in him.

In the first days, one expected the quietly flickering flame of life to go out every hour. But then it seemed as if the struggle could drag on. After feverish excitement, quiet times came when the injured man's mind was clear.

Shaken, Dr. Goebbels sat next to his most loyal comrade-in-arms and looked, full of pain, into the once-beautiful young man's face, disfigured by a nefarious hand. Only from the eyes did the strong spirit of the young German hero shine out at him in his usual familiarity. "I am so happy," came a whisper from the dry, fever-cracked lips, and the handshake told the doctor that the brave fighter still believed in victory over death—strong and conscious of victory until his last breath.

And then came days when hope for a cure also made the doctors happy. The tongue, split lengthwise by the bullet, was healing and usable again. With a grateful spirit, Dr. Goebbels saw the brave boy sitting upright on the pillows during his next visit and was able to talk to him. With the passionate sympathy that always animated him, Horst heard him speak of the successes that had come to the movement and of the battles he had fought with the enemy. His faith in victory continued even on the bed of wounds. How deeply his spirit was connected to everything concerning the movement, despite the pains and hardships, was best demonstrated by his support for the admission of Prince August Wilhelm of Prussia. People were suspicious of the prince and feared that the admission of a Hohenzollern offspring would harm the movement. But Horst Wessel had recognized from the loyal, selfless nature of the prince's cooperation that he was professing National Socialism out of a serious, honest will, and urgently asked for admission to the party.

"Whether prince or worker, it is the same. With the same right that we grant to the converted Red Front member, an emperor's son may also put on the brown shirt. Go and talk to the Führer."

With these words Horst Wessel once again laid out the case. And the doctor promised to work as wished for by the wounded fighter.

*

Another scene: Horst Wessel lies in the pillows with his head bandaged. From the bed of pain his shining eyes greet the SA comrades who quietly wave past the open door to prove their love and solidarity to the *Sturmführer* and hero.

All of Germany, insofar as it is inspired by national sentiments, takes the deepest interest in the fate of this German youth who was attacked by nefarious bandits. Joy reigns everywhere, even in national German circles abroad, at the hopeful prospect of the brave fighter's recovery.

Only the sinister ones in the communist camp rage, and a slobbering wave of hatred sparks up when they learn that a spark of hope has been kindled to preserve this young life. The perpetrators make themselves at home in the villas and country houses of the red leaders, and are eventually sent abroad with false passports. They had done their duty. Now it was the turn of the red media. They poured their foul-mouthed hatred on the young hero and tried to portray him as a degenerate. Even the social-democratic papers backed away from this disgraceful deed, and a storm of indignation arose in the left-wing bourgeois press because of such low mendacity.

But the agitation of the communist newspapers provoked a new outrage. One of the red cliques decided to storm pavilion seven, where Horst Wessel was lying, and to finish off the hated Nazi leader with hand grenades. The inhuman plan would have succeeded if someone's conscience hadn't got the better of him and forced him to write a letter to the family informing them of the shameful attack. Inge immediately called *Staf*4, who rushed to Friedrichshain with his men and sharply confronted the jeering mob. Even if they felt hindered in carrying out their reprehensible attack, everyone should see how it was in their dark hearts, and savage shouts rang out into the silence of the hospital. "Go to hell, Nazi!" screamed the mob, stripped of all human emotion.

The news of the deterioration in the condition of the SA fighter Horst Wessel, who was struggling for light and life, hit all well-meaning people with the full force of a setback after the glimmer of hope.

Despairing under the powerlessness of their craft, the doctors stood at the bedside of the brave man whom they would so desperately have liked to preserve for the German people and for a promising life. Everything was going so well, when blood-poisoning occurred, against which all of their skill was powerless. All of them who worked around him in their nursing profession felt painfully and depressingly their helplessness in the face of this devastating turn of events.

Just as the German-minded in all districts of the Reich had expressed their joy at the recovery through broadcasts and congratulations, so now they expressed their grief.

Horst Wessel had to undergo the last operation.

He grasps the doctor's hands and begs, "Stay with me!" and Dr. Goebbels stays, although he was to speak at a large meeting in the Sportpalast. Nothing in life is as important to him as this beloved German boy.

Fever dreams take hold of his mind again, whisking him far away into the circles of his SA comrades, whose names glide across his lips.

Then his mind regains its clarity and he says to the nurse, "Sister, I've had a wonderful life after all!" And then with reference to the freedom movement he is carried off: "Now it's inexorably on to victory!"

He knows that he can no longer escape death, and says wistfully to his sister, "Inge dear, now you must do for me what you did for Werner."

Then the last night of the battle dawns with all of its grueling struggle and no faith in victory. Outside around pavilion seven stands Storm 5 and many from other storms. They want to hope, and cannot find the courage; but close they want to be to their fellow fighter—their best!

On stockings some creep in, standing at the door. In a bright moment, his gaze falls on them. He recognizes them, smiles once more and whispers, "Look, Inge, how faithful they are!"

As morning dawns, his lips breathe once more, "Dear Mother. . . . Dear Inge. . . ."

Softly he slumbers away into another life without struggle. Horst Wessel has left this world for a better one.

Here Mournful Love; There Poisonous Hatred

Horst Wessel, the fighter, had stopped breathing, but the battle-air still wafted around the dear dead man.

The law asserted their rights over him, and only after a long negotiation did his mother receive her dead son. Storm 1 has arrived, SA men carry the coffin to the car, escorted by heavily armed *Schupo* men in police cars, as if he, who died for Germany's freedom, were a dangerous threat to the country.

He lies laid out in the brown room of his parents' apartment. He rests so peacefully among flowers as never before in his turbulent life as a fighter. A stream of people and flowers poured into the house on the Jüdenstraße. Everyone, regardless of rank and age, wants to show their support for the sacrifice for liberation from bondage. School-children and students, citizens and peasants, workers and civil servants, young soldiers and old front-line fighters: the German heart drives them all to the bier of the young German hero, just like people make a pilgrimage to their most sacred altar.

Silent, their hearts torn with pain, their souls constricted by a dull pressure of grief, the men of Storm 5 stand and keep vigil at the bier of their leader.

He is to be given a dignified burial. Inge Wessel fights for this; it is as if she has a mission to fulfill. She rushes from one authority to another, from office to office—everywhere she is listened to with the greatest politeness, but in all offices her request for a cemetery escort worthy of her brother is met with the same cold-hearted rejection. Nowhere is there understanding, nowhere respect for death and the dead. Petty revenge, lowly spite deny the dead hero the last tribute of a special honor. People hide behind fears of great unrest. The gentlemen explain with great regret that they are responsible for order in the city and should not provoke the already agitated masses even more by approving a large funeral procession.

Inge, in whom something of her dead brother's militant spirit has awakened, threatens that she will turn to the *Reichspräsident* in case of further refusals. So she gets through to the police chief, and when he says something about "civil war" in connection to her brother's funeral, she answers him straightforwardly that his ban on the funeral procession is creating unrest and civil war, because the militant youth of Berlin and the whole Reich want to escort their murdered brother to his grave. She then takes out a large sheet of paper and holds it before the astonished gentleman's eyes. There are all the associations that have approached the family with the request to participate in the funeral procession.

Now the eyes of the police chief open, but also the seed sprouts up which Horst Wessel's sacrificial death has caused to take root in German hearts. With dismay, the Lord recognizes that beyond divisive details, Horst Wessel's violent death has called and united the German national associations like a flaming beacon. But precisely in the face of this overwhelming fact, the police authorities persist in their rejectionist stance. All that Inge can achieve is that seven—a total of seven—passenger cars are permitted as a funeral procession, and that the Normannia and Alemannia representatives, about a dozen people, are allowed to join the procession, dressed in all their clothes and with flags unfurled. All other associations are not allowed to take part in the funeral procession, but they may attend the ceremony in the cemetery.

The enemies pursue the dead hero to the grave and deny him the respect that an enemy who fought so chivalrously deserves. In doing so, they have judged themselves.

Time moves on relentlessly, and the hour comes when Horst Wessel is to be laid to rest. SA men and *Korps* members in complete dress stand rigid and serious next to the coffin covered with a swastika flag, on which also lie the *Korps* caps and the *Sturmführer* cap.

After the short funeral service inside, the *Sturmführer* of Standard 4 carries the coffin out. But a police lieutenant appears and demands in a gruff tone that the swastika flag, the banner of German freedom under which Horst Wessel fought and fell, be removed from the coffin.

Excitement seizes the young people. After a futile attempt at mediation by the priests, Inge Wessel, with a threatening gleam in her eyes, orders the lieutenant out and has wreaths made with wire around the sacred banner, the battle emblem of the dead man. The banner sacred to the dead man must be hidden under flowers.

Solemn silence reigns as the coffin is carried off. Slowly the small procession starts to move, uniforms all around. A crowd of police guard the German hero on his last march—as the hateful spirit of the enemy wanted it. He is buried with a police detachment, but his mighty spirit, which rose from the open tomb and flew far and wide through the German countryside to call upon German hearts, could not be stopped by a chain of *Schupo* men!

The procession passes through a few quiet streets full of densely packed crowds waiting in reverent silence. But then, at the corner of the Weidingerstraße and Lothringerstraße, the communists have seized the post, and a hellish noise roars towards the humble procession. Shouts greet them, and a hail of stones pelts the wagons, whose windows shatter into pieces. The street has been officially closed to the faithful of German blood from all national associations, but the police chief has opened it to the mob, the riffraff of the underworld—to insult the purified dead. The German name has never been more disgraced than by the stones thrown and the attacks of an inhuman mob on Horst Wessel's funeral procession. And those who brought this about in tacit tolerance as decreeing officials, they were close in spirit to that wild crowd.

Never Forget This, German Youth

A few streets away, another stone salvo pelts the funeral procession and shots ring out. The red hordes break through the police cordon, attack the students, and try to snatch the *Korps* flag. But then they reach the wrong side, make the acquaintance of the steel blades, and flee with bleeding heads after Ede Weiß has rushed to the rescue with the Eighth Storm.

Armored cars rattle up, and after a short street battle the procession is able to continue. Sad salvos rattle through the streets on the way to Horst Wessel's grave. Fighting to the grave was Horst Wessel's life.

Finally, the ordeal is over for the two women. They have reached the entrance to the cemetery. Another attempt by the red gang to advance was nipped in the bud by the SA.

The Flags Are Lowered

An incalculable crowd fills the cemetery. Head to head they stand, SA, Stahlhelm, Korps members, and others from a hundred different associations, to honor the cruelly murdered freedom fighter, and to publicly declare their solidarity with him.

Solemn silence falls over the thousands, hearts full of respect and grief, as mother and sister walk behind the coffin.

Wrapped in the beloved banner, the earthly shell of the dead man sinks into the tomb. After the priest delivers his eulogy, Captain von Pfeffer, the *OSAF*, approaches the grave and lays a wreath in the name of the afflicted Führer, Hitler. Heartfelt words of farewell are dedicated to the dead friend and comrade. Captain Göring throws the storm cap into the grave after the dead man, and the students do the same with his *Korps* bands and caps.

Then Dr. Goebbels is the last to approach the grave. It is not, as usual, a fiery, ravishing speech that blazes from his eloquent lips. No, he speaks to the deceased as his best and most loyal friend, closely connected to him in spirit and deed. But his words sound all the more moving; they touch the hearts of the faithful. The March wind softly rustles its accompanying melody in the old elms and the flowing banners.

He says, "And when the SA is summoned for the last roll call, then they will also call your name, Comrade Wessel! And all, all SA men will answer: 'here!' Because the SA—that is Horst Wessel!"

That is the great unifying word.

Further on, the doctor finds prophetic words of endless storms that would march, and of swastika flags waving over free German lands. They have come true; we have all experienced the great uprising in the German spirit and see in Adolf Hitler the appointed leader of the whole German nation at work. The promise in Horst Wessel's song "Die Fahne Hoch" has come true!

Dr. Goebbels shouts one last farewell into the grave of his faithful comrade, then *Staf* 4 raises his hand. Once again the flags are lowered, a roaring last greeting to the faithful SA *Sturmführer*, and the drums roll muffled with lamentation.

Then the words resound far and wide above the crowd: "*Ich hatt' einen Kameraden, einen bessern findst du nit."*[36]

The celebration is over. Crowds stream away into Berlin. But the way home is not without disturbances. Fights between SA, Stahlhelm, students, and the red cliques break out in various places until the police, who are at first at a loss, proceed ruthlessly and bludgeon anything and everything that gets in their way.

That was the bitter end of Horst Wessel's funeral day. How the heart of the tortured mother must have bled when the wild screams of the street fight reached her during the drive home. How infinitely shameful in view of the pure and clear ideal figure of her dead child, glowing with noble devotion and love for the people.

It took a long time for the deeply-saddened mother's heart to find surrender and clear peace. She drew new strength and fortitude for her life from the countless letters that poured into her quiet home from the Reich and other countries of the wide globe in a steadily swelling flood. All of them, without exception, expressed their boundless respect for the devoted work of her beloved son for the freedom of Germany, combined with deep sorrow over his tragic sacrificial death. Such good this did the mother! Out of all these heartfelt outpourings rose the image of her son, pure, good, and brave. Then she realized that she had given the German people a hero and the German youth a role model whose memory will be preserved as long as the German language knows how to tell of the heroes of our people.

The fighter with the German heart now rests in the cool earth. But the wave of hatred also wanted to reach this sacred place. Even the desecration of the grave was not shied away from by the corrupted, blinded Red Front. Again it was the faithful SA who guarded the grave of their fallen comrade by day and by night with the loyalty that they had learned from him and protected it from defilement and destruction. In the communist newspapers the spiteful defilement of the dead freedom fighter continued without any authority daring to take action against the spreaders of these lies. It was not until the day of liberation on January 30th, 1933 was heralded by the ringing of iron bells that this venomous mouth fell silent—forever.

The winds carry the songs of the liberated German people over Horst Wessel's grave in the Nikolai cemetery in Berlin. Free of any

---

[36] "I once had a comrade, you won't find a better one."

non-German essence is the earth in whose sacred bosom he rests. But we know: he is not dead; his spirit marches along in our ranks. He is everywhere where Hitler-flags flutter in National Socialist Germany.

Sacrifices are sacred and obligatory. But you, German youth, show yourself worthy of this sublime example, for it was for you foremost that he died. His blood was shed for your future! Let Horst Wessel's spirit work in your actions for the prosperity and blossoming of the people and Fatherland for whose liberation he died.

Heroes' names are written in the sky. But the name of Horst Wessel shines in the German sky like an eternal star—as long as you, German youth, remain loyal to him!

HORST WESSEL: THROUGH STORM AND STRUGGLE TO IMMORTALITY

MAX KULLAK

Dedicated to my SA Storm 22/98

Horst Wessel at the head of his Storm 5
Nuremberg 1929

ADMITTANCE TO THE STURMABTEILUNG

Wir sind des Hitler braune Sturmkolonnen,
Wir führen stolz das Hakenkreuzpanier,
Wir haben kühn den Kampf ums Recht begonnen,
Wir künden's froh, das Dritte Reich sind wir.
Wohlan, wohl mögt ihr uns bekämpfen,
Ihr könnt die Glut nicht dämpfen;
Mit uns der Sieg, mit uns das Feldgeschrei:
Deutschland erwache! Deutschland, du bist frei!

Im roten Feld, auf strahlend weißem Grunde
Lacht uns der Väter heilig Sonnenkreuz.
Wir alle fühlen unsers Volkes Stunde:
Der Herrgott will es und die Pflicht gebeut's!
Und mögen wir auch sterben,
Wir schaffen unsern Erben ein neues Reich.
Drum bleibt das Feldgeschrei:
Deutschland erwache! Deutschland, du bist frei!

We are Hitler's brown Stormtroopers,
We proudly carry the swastika,
We have boldly started the fight for justice,
We joyfully proclaim that we are the Third Reich.
Well, well, you may fight us,
You cannot dim the flame;
With us the victory, with us the battle cry:
Germany awake! Germany, you are free!

On a red patch, on a shining white base
The holy sun cross of the fathers smiles at us.
We all feel our people's hour:
The Lord God wills it and duty dictates it!
And even if we die,
We'll create a new empire for our heirs.
Therefore the battle cry remains:
Germany awake! Germany, you are free!

It is an autumn afternoon in 1926. The student Horst Wessel is standing in his room in the Jüdenstraße in Berlin and proudly looks at himself. For the first time he is wearing the uniform of the SA, the dress of honor of the Sturmabteilung of his leader Adolf Hitler. Today is the storm evening meeting of Storm 2, which he has joined. In the evening, some SA comrades will pick him up, because it is not wise for a newcomer to walk alone from the vicarage in the Jüdenstraße to the storm pub in a brown uniform. Lurking in the narrow streets are the communist bands, savage figures, armed with clubs, daggers, and revolvers, ready to cowardly attack lone Nazis. They feel strong enough to beat the "Hitler bandits," the "brown plague," who want to take the streets away from them.

Someone knocks on the door of his room. "Hold on a moment, mother," Horst shouts, "you'll be able to see and admire me in a moment!" Quickly he puts on the belt and the shoulder straps and puts on his cap. Then Horst opens the door and lets his mother enter. Pastor Wessel's wife takes just one look at the brown uniform and a shock goes through her. She immediately knows the dangerous path her eldest son is about to take, as she reads about the attacks on National Socialists in the newspaper almost every day. But not a word of condemnation crosses her lips. She knows the compelling power of the uniform, which demands duty and sacrifice. Such was the case in August 1914, when her husband, the pastor Dr. Ludwig Wessel, put on his uniform and took leave to go into service. And so she once again imagined before her the many young volunteers of 1914 from her acquaintance in uniform. Yes, she knew the power of the uniform. Horst had already worn the uniform of the Black *Reichswehr* at the age of sixteen and had been trained in military service instead of taking a vacation. After his discharge from the army, he wore the uniform of the Bismarck League as a first-year student, and one year later the uniform of the military organization Wiking under Captain Ehrhardt. But those had all been harmless soldiering games. Now, she feels in her mother's heart, now it is getting serious, now her Horst is a soldier of Adolf Hitler in his new brown uniform; now it is a matter of life and death, just like in 1914. And then the song of the soldier's farewell from the Great War comes to her mind:

Laß mich gehn, Mutter, laß mich gehn!
All das Weinen kann uns nichts mehr nützen;
Denn wir gehn, das Vaterland zu schützen.
Laß mich gehn, Mutter, laß mich gehn!
Deinen letzten Gruß will ich vom Mund dir küssen:
Deutschland muß leben, und wenn wir sterben müssen!

Let me go, Mother, let me go!
Crying won't do us any good any more;
for we go to protect the fatherland.
Let me go, mother, let me go!
Your last greeting I will kiss from your mouth:
Germany must live, even if we must die!

"Mother," Horst exclaims, "look, I can't help it. I have now found the right thing to do; I am proud to be a National Socialist and to fight for the Third Reich!" His sister Inge and brother Werner enter the room. Werner's gaze rests contemplatively on the swastika armband on his brother's arm. It will only be a short time until he is a member of the Sturmabteilung like his brother Horst.

Darkness has fallen. A whistle sounds in front of the house. Horst's SA comrades are downstairs and want to pick him up. They walk through dark alleys while the people of Rotmord stand in doorways and gateways,[37] their faces contorted with hatred, their fists in their pockets. Nothing happens; only when Horst passes by with his people do they start shouting, "Nazi dogs! To hell with Hitler! Traitors to the workers!"—traitors to the workers? Horst Wessel couldn't get these words off his mind; after all, Hitler called his movement the National Socialist German Workers' Party. Who was actually betraying the worker, and who was doing right by him?

---

[37] Red Murder

Yes, who actually were his workers? Were they the ones who were doing road-work in the street in front of them? Wasn't the cobbler also working in the shop on the left, or the baker working over there? And wasn't he himself working in his books? Had not his father worked at his sermons and through spiritual guidance? He had to gain complete clarity about these things; perhaps then he could better understand the inexplicable hatred and thus help to overcome it.

In front of them was the storm pub of Storm 2. It was a miserable pub with a sober interior. Two SA men stood guard in front of it because they had often been attacked by the reds. They entered the hall with the Hitler-salute. The storm was almost completely present. Curious glances were directed at him, for word had already spread that a newcomer was coming today: one who had an education; a student. There were not many of them in the SA at that time. Would he get along with all those who looked toward him? Would he be able to be their SA comrade in life and death? A combat song was sung: rough and coarse. The *Sturmführer* welcomed him with simple, cordial words; it was not at all solemn and touching. The duty roster was then discussed. What struck Horst immediately was the discipline and the stiff posture when one spoke to the *Sturmführer*. It reminded him of his time as a soldier in the Black *Reichswehr*, where everyone had to obey the leader without question. Then they talked about Adolf Hitler and about the new *Gauleiter*, Dr. Goebbels, who with his fiery eloquence got to grips with even the roughest among them—and lo and behold, the new guy was not at all proud and pretentious; he could talk to them in the Berlin dialect; he was a fine fellow who could talk to them about their hardships and also had a crude wit. Some sat closer to him and listened. Then the *Sturmführer* spoke again, making Adolf Hitler's aims clear to them, and when it was time to leave, some stood by the newcomer: "Horst, we're taking you home!" The first bond of solidarity was forged. Even here, Horst's gift of being a comrade, of understanding the common man and drawing him in, was evident. They brought their youngest SA comrade home to the Jüdenstraße without any trouble.

NATIONAL SOCIALISM

Heraus, verführte Volksgenossen,
Aus roter Front und Reaktion,
Kämpft mit gemeinsam und geschlossen
Für den Sieg der deutschen Revolution.
Reiht euch ein in Hitlers Sturmkolonnen,
Kämpft für Freiheit, Brot und Recht.
Schon hat der letzte Kampf begonnen
Für ein neues Arbeitssgeschlecht.

Nationaler Sozialismus
Kämpft für Arbeit, Freiheit, Brot.
Nationaler Sozialismus
Führt uns einst aus dieser Not. (x2)

Get out, seduced community members,
Of the Red Front and reaction,
Fight together and as one
For the victory of the German revolution.
Join Hitler's storm columns,
Fight for freedom, bread and justice.
The final struggle has already begun
For a new labor law.

National Socialism
Fights for work, freedom, bread.
National Socialism
Will one day lead us out of this misery. (x2)

Horst Wessel could not sleep that night. The *Sturmführer's* words about Adolf Hitler's National Socialism kept running through his head. National: yes, that's what he had always been; for him it meant as much as being militant, brave, and fighting for Germany when it was required. His father had also been national in his work during the war and in his preaching. Many of his mother's acquaintances, mostly retired officers and civil servants, called themselves national. Often, during visits, he heard one of them say "we must have the good old days again, like before the war; there's nothing like a vigorous military march!" And then the old gentleman would stand up and take a few steps around the room with his legs stiff. Again and again he came back to the old days when the officer and the civil servant alone gave orders, when they lived in strict seclusion and only talked to their own kind, or sat with their own kind at the regulars' table. And each time the conversation ended with a rant about the new era, about the workers who had brought about the revolution, and those who were far too well off. This talk often seemed to Horst Wessel, who was after all a child of the new era, like the dusty plush curtains on the windows and doors of those retired gentlemen. Horst could do nothing with their eternal retrospective view, with their one-sided claims to power, or with their arrogance and their titles—they called it all "national spirit." These must have been the groups that brought down Adolf Hitler's freedom movement in Munich on November 9th, 1923 out of envious lust for power. Horst was sixteen years old at the time and did not understand why old officers who called themselves "national" had allowed National Socialists to be shot. By this time in his life, he understood the meaning of the song the SA sang; he knew what "*Reaktion*" meant in that song of the dead of November 9th, 1923:

In München sind viele gefallen,
In München war'n viele dabei,
Es traf vor der Feldherrnhalle
Deutsche Helden das tödliche Blei.
Sie kämpften für Deutschlands Erwachen
Im Glauben an Hitlers Mission!
Marschierten mit Todesverachten
In das Feuer der Reaktion!

In Munich many have fallen,
In Munich many were there,
It hit in front of the Feldherrnhalle[38]
German heroes the deadly bullet.
They fought for Germany's awakening
With faith in Hitler's mission!
Marched with contempt for death
Into the fire of reaction!

But the military associations he joined, the Bismarck League and the Wiking, also called themselves "national." Certainly, strict military discipline and order prevailed; they were educated in military service and love for the Fatherland, as well as in obedience and the fulfillment of duty. He particularly liked the Wiking under Captain Ehrhardt and the song they sang:

Hakenkreuz am Stahlhelm,	Swastika on the Stahlhelm,
Schwarzweißrot das Band.	The ribbon black, white and red.
Die Brigade Ehrhardt	The Ehrhardt Brigade[39]
Werden wir genannt.	We are called.

He liked what they called "national" among the young comrades there. But who were his comrades? They were all young people from his own background: pupils and students—in any case all educated people; boys from workers', craftsmen's, and peasants' communities were not among them. So was being "national" tied to better backgrounds and clothing? It almost seemed so.

Horst Wessel had the same experience with his fellow Corps members and life in the Normannia Corps in Berlin. All of them were splendid young people from a good family, nationally minded, ready to defend themselves in bloody *mensur*,[40] reliable, and loyal. But why were they national and not the many young people from other

---

[38] The Feldherrnhalle was the scene of a confrontation on Friday morning, November 9th, 1923, between the Bavarian State Police and the followers of Adolf Hitler in which the Nazi party attempted to storm the Bavarian Defense Ministry, commonly referred to as the Beer Hall Putsch.
[39] The Marine brigade Ehrhardt was a *Freikorps* group of around six thousand men formed by Lieutenant-Commander Hermann Ehrhardt in the aftermath of World War I. The Marine brigade Ehrardt was involved in the Kapp-Lüttwitz Putsch, an attempted coup against the Weimar government in Berlin on March 13th, 1920.
[40] Fencing duels.

backgrounds? Was being national a characteristic of the upper classes after all? Or had the common people just somehow lost their national identity? During the war, Father had told them that the common soldiers had fought with just as much national enthusiasm. What had happened to their national identity now? Most of them were with the communists, with the Red Front or in the Reichsbanner, and there was no bridge between the nationalist people in his circles and the common people. Or was there?

He thought of that night's storm evening meeting. There he, the student, and a few more people from his circles had been together with roadworkers, bricklayers, chauffeurs, trash collectors, and shop assistants. They all understood each other without many words. They didn't hate each other and they only had two goals: to help Adolf Hitler and to form a large German national community, no matter what profession the individual had. These National Socialists were national; they loved Germany, and fought and bled for it. They were national, although they were for the most part ordinary people. Everyone was welcome to them, whether upper or lower class, if only they fought with them for Adolf Hitler, and they called such people "community members," offered them their hand, and recruited them. At that storm evening meeting it had become quite clear to Horst Wessel why Adolf Hitler called his movement National Socialism. Being national was not enough; one also had to be social, to see the community member in every decent German and respect him. Why did the reds hate them so much instead of coming to them in large numbers and becoming equally respected community members? Why did the educated and the bourgeois despise the Nazis, considering them to be ruffians with whom they wanted nothing to do? They were both misguided, uprooted from the national community; it was essential to help them, to call out to them, "Come out, misguided community members; come out of the Red Front and reaction!"

SA SERVICE

Durchs Groß-Berlin marschieren wir.
Für Adolf Hitler kämpfen wir!
Die rote Front, brecht sie entzweit
SA. marschiert—Achtung—die Straße frei!

So stehen wir im Kampf allein,
Durch Blut geschweißt sind unsere Reih'n.
Den Blick nach vorn, die Faust geballt!
Die Straße laut von unserm Schritt erschallt.

Und ist der Kampf auch noch so schwer,
Wir wanken, weichen nimmermehr.
Wir fordern Freiheit, Recht und Brot,
Für Deutschlands Zukunft geh'n wir in den Tod.

Through Greater Berlin we march.[41]
For Adolf Hitler we fight!
The Red Front, break it apart
SA marches—attention—clear the street!

So we stand alone in the struggle
Our ranks are welded by blood.
Our eyes forward, our fists clenched!
The streets resonate loudly with our footsteps.

---

[41] Greater Berlin refers to Berlin and the surrounding towns and rural communities. In 1920, the Prussian government passed the Greater Berlin Act, thus officially creating the region.

No matter how hard the battle
We'll never waver, we'll never flinch
We demand freedom, justice and bread
For Germany's future we go to our deaths.[42]

Months have since passed and Horst Wessel is now an SA man, heart and soul. Why continue with his studies now? He is gifted; he will catch up quickly later: thusly he comforts himself and his mother. What is the point of the fencing and cheerful activities of his fellow Corps members? They are clueless; don't they know that the murderous communists will soon attack them with more lethal weapons? Do none of them think of the gruesome mass-murders of the citizens of Russia? He sees the terrible danger for Germany. The SA will awaken the sleeping community members; it will fight and sacrifice itself.

The SA calls the roll at the Jüdenhof; the Second Storm lines up. The *Sturmführer* announces that there will be a publicity march through Wedding, a wicked communist district in the north of Berlin. "I expect iron discipline from you. Don't get agitated; everyone stays in line. We want to show the red thugs that the SA keeps discipline and order and does not fear those hiding there in their hideouts. Turn to the right. In-step, march!" The swastika flag is in front, the men march three by three next to each other with the storm straps under their chins. Horst Wessel is among them. A roar goes up all around the Jüdenhof: "To hell with the Nazis! Down with the brown dogs!" and in-between, again and again, there is the cry "Red Front!" The communists who live in this old part of town at Jüdenhof and close by in Fischerkietz shout out their rage that German community members dare to contest the street with them, the mercenaries of Moscow. The march goes on, burning with hatred and murderous desire. In Wedding the communists are accompanied by the police, who are supposed to be protecting German community members in the capital of the German Reich from the emissaries and deceivers of Moscow! Stones and beer bottles fly into the marching line; the first drops of blood flow from the faces of those struck, but the march continues. The spiteful shouts of the opponents are drowned out by

---

[42] This song has the same melody as the "*Argonnerwaldlied,*" a German military march from World War I.

two powerful shouts that resound for the first time ever in this red area: "Heil Hitler!" and "Germany, awake!" Horst Wessel gets his baptism of fire, but he clearly sees his task before him: to break the red terror, to make the deceived community members into German people again, and to redeem them from the curse of incitement and from misery, from housing shortages and unemployment. They should not sing the "*Internationale*," but the "*Deutschlandlied*." They should, finally, Horst Wessel wished, wake up and realize that no foreign country, no collective conscience, no *Internationale* can help them, but only Germany alone and the leader of the Germany-to-be, Adolf Hitler.

SA service: Horst learns about another means of recruitment. One evening in the storm pub, the *Sturmführer* distributes posters and calls for a meeting in which the opponents are also to be given the freedom to speak. Now the posters have to be stuck up so that they shine and advertise far and wide. They set out at night in groups of four or five people with poster-rollers, paintbrushes, and a pot of paste. They have to be careful: enemy columns are on their way; often there are fights and shootings at poster walls, fences, and street corners, and afterwards they are arrested by the police and interrogated for hours. Others receive instructions from the *Sturmführer* to distribute them on the streets and in the buildings, especially in the red neighborhoods. These SA comrades are told to start distributing under the eaves, so that in the event of a clash the way past the lower apartments would still be clear. Horst Wessel experiences all of this. What was it like to distribute leaflets on the street? One could get to know people and gain experience. Once he stood with a fellow in front of a brightly-lighted gourmet restaurant on the Kurfürstendamm. Plump racketeers in their fur coats and top hats and their ladies came and went here while many hundreds of thousands of community members were starving. If one offered them a note, they turned around or grumbled in flawed German about being harassed and called for the police—or they stood in front of a respectable pub where the citizens bowled or had their regular drink. Then they came out, fat and cheerful, to go home. If one offered them a note, they sometimes took it, but almost always said the same thing: "Leave me alone with politics; I want my peace and my sleep!" Some of them who reluctantly took a note were soon surprised that their own son came home one day in the brown uniform. Thus Horst Wessel got to know two other kinds of people besides the Red Front people and the reactionaries, the racketeer and the uncaring philistine. What enormous tasks lie ahead of him: overcoming all of this resistance to form a national community, as Adolf Hitler wanted it.

SA service: in a smoky hall in the old town there is a publicity meeting of the NSDAP. Dr. Goebbels is to speak. The Second Storm provides security. The hall is filled long before the start. Horst Wessel looks around. But they are not all supporters here! He sees a lot of familiar faces from the communists. The tall man there with the stiff, black hat over his forehead, he lives in the Jüdenhof, he shouted at him the other day, "To hell with the Nazis!" And he sees many other opponents; they have spread out across the hall and are quiet for the time being. But what will happen when Dr. Goebbels speaks? First they let him speak calmly, then there is a heavy bang; a communist has fired a gun, and now the roaring and whistling starts. The hall guards gather close in front of the speaker's desk to catch the beer glasses and mugs that are being hurled. But now the melee begins against a crowd five times their size. The storm takes the speaker in its midst and fights its way out; blood flows, bones are broken, but everyone has made it through!

Guarding the room: SA service! So the SA man Horst Wessel takes part in everything: the scouting of enemy meetings, marches and truck rides to the countryside and the surrounding towns, jiu-jitsu exercises to repel the enemy, and errands from the *Sturmführer* to the *Gau* and to the localities.[43] He learns everything from scratch and he knows that's how it has to be. If he wants to help and lead later on he must learn to serve and obey.

---

[43] A *Gau* is like a province.

PUBLICITY TRIP TO PASEWALK

Kameraden, laßt erschallen ein sturmgewaltig Lied.
Den Helden soll es hallen, verstreut in Nord und Süd,
Im Osten und im Westen, wo Hitlers Fahne weht.
Ja, wir zählen zu den Besten, solang die Treu besteht.
Und sieht man uns, so sagt man, wenn wir vorüberziehen:
Das sind die Hitlerleute, vom ersten Sturm Berlin.

Comrades, let a powerful song resound.
Let it be heard by the heroes, scattered in North and South,
In East and West, where Hitler's flag waves.
Yes, we are among the best, as long as loyalty remains.
And when they see us, they say, when we pass by:
These are the Hitler people, from the 1st Storm of Berlin.

"Now let's practice that again right away! Go! I'll accompany it!"
Storm 1, in which Horst Wessel and his brother Werner were then
serving, was gathered tightly around the piano in the storm pub,
where Horst was sitting. Singing was fun for everyone; that's when
people noticed, when it sounded so neat during the marches, that
National Socialism was marching forward victoriously. And this
song was composed by their Horst Wessel, who also wrote the
melody. All the stanzas were sung with vigor. Tomorrow, the SA
comrades and the residents of Pasewalk would be amazed when they
marched into the small town behind Pomerania with the new song!
Sturmführer Sprengel then assigned them all to the trucks and
discussed the order of the trucks and the march to Pasewalk itself.
Then they sat together and talked. "What kind of a place is Pasewalk?
You know all about that, don't you, Horst?" He pondered. Should
he tell them what his father had told him about the proud past of the
Pasewalk cuirassiers? That they had emerged from the glorious
Bayreuth dragoon regiment that won the battle of Hohenfriedberg for

Frederick the Great and captured sixty-six flags? But no, the Pasewalk cuirassiers no longer existed; according to the Treaty of Versailles, there was only one mounted regiment in Pasewalk. But he could tell them something else. It was there in Pasewalk that the first thoughts of the National Socialist movement had been conceived. It was there, shortly after the war, that the Führer Adolf Hitler lay in a field hospital as a simple soldier, temporarily blinded by English gas grenades. There the helpless man wept over the disgrace of the revolution, over the humiliation and disintegration of Germany; there the thought of Germany's salvation may have risen in him: the thought he took with him to Munich and continued to advocate for in a tough struggle. There in Pasewalk, in the place where Adolf Hitler had suffered physically and mentally, they wanted to campaign and fight for him.

Shaken by the long night's journey on the trucks, Storm 1 arrived in Pasewalk at dawn. But all tiredness had disappeared. Horst Wessel's new song rang out joyfully to greet the forty Pasewalk SA members who had marched to meet them outside the town. But they also heard hateful shouts of "Red Front!" when they arrived at the market square; there they saw familiar faces from the streets of Berlin again. The worst and most audacious communist troops from Berlin had been called in against Storm 1. That could result in more bloodshed!

They had hardly gathered in the safe house when the first bit of bad news came: the communists had attacked the trucks and the weak SA guard on top of them in large numbers. After a short shootout, the police and the *Landjäger* had intervened. But instead of keeping the communists away from the building, the police retreated, and now the encirclement and siege of the Nazis by the communists began. A fierce firefight with pistols commenced. There were minor and major injuries on both sides. Then the word came that the communists were preparing to storm the safe house. Immediately, *Sturmführer* Sprengel had barricades built from tables, chairs, and barrels, behind which his men hacked and lay and fought back. Finally the police intervened again; they drove the reds away but attacked the SA men. Finally the hated Nazis were to be dealt with, who, as the police officers were repeatedly told, were a bunch of dangerous thugs. "*Sturmführer!*" one of them suddenly shouted, "there, the cannon in the courtyard, that'll be fun!" They actually grabbed the spokes of the old cannon—it had no breechblock and belonged to the Pasewalk War Association—and set it up in front of the gate, which they suddenly opened. The police left in a hurry. But then the mayor called a squadron of the cavalry regiment to help against the evil Nazis. When they appeared with their *Rittmeister*, the *Sturmführer* immediately realized that resistance was futile. "SA, assemble!" rang out the command. All those who were healthy or slightly wounded lined up. They were all checked for weapons, but no pistol was found. *Sturmführer* Sprengel—Barrikadenalbert was his nickname from then on—and his adjutant Horst Wessel were not examined because they were the leaders; they had hidden the collected pistols in boots, bags, bread bags, and brown shirts. The *Rittmeister* granted them a free pass. They went home in a victorious spirit. They had bled in Pasewalk, but they had shown that Adolf Hitler's movement was growing and fighting. Berlin brought the usual surprise. Horst Wessel and his trucks were stopped by the police and arrested. Sprengel, on the other hand, had travelled by train with the wounded, but had already gotten off in a suburb. What did it matter to the SA men to spend a few days sitting in the Alex, the police headquarters? They were used to that. That's exactly how Horst Wessel felt. The comrades told his mother, and he had time there to think deeply and thoroughly about the SA's struggle, or to write a new song. The main thing he wanted was for the movement to grow and gain loyal followers. There he also thought about how to approach the deceived community members, what he would have to say to them, how he could make Adolf Hitler's thoughts clear to them, and how he could draw them to him. Horst Wessel's eloquence, inherited from his father, was soon to become apparent.

AMONG THE PEOPLE

Es pfeift von allen Dächern für heut die Arbeit aus,
Es ruhen die Maschinen, wir gehen jetzt nach Haus.
Daheim ist Not und Elend, das ist der Arbeit Lohn.
Geduld, Verratene Brüder, schon wanket Judas Thron.

Geduld und ballt die Fäuste, sie hören nicht den Sturm,
Sie hören nicht sein Brausen und nicht die Glock' vom Turm';
Sie kennen nicht den Hunger, sie hören nicht den Schrei,
Gebt Raum der deutschen Arbeit, für uns die Straße frei!

Ein Hoch der deutschen Arbeit, voran die Fahne rot,
Das Hakenkreuz muß siegen, vom Freiheitslicht umloht.
Es kämpfen deutsche Männer für eine neue Zeit,
Wir wollen nicht ruh'n noch rasten, bis Deutschland einst befreit.

The whistle blows from every rooftop for today's work,
The machines are at rest, we're going home now.
At home is hardship and misery; that is the reward of labor.
Patience, betrayed brothers, Judas' throne is already shaking.

Patience and clench your fists, they hear not the storm,
They do not hear its roar, they do not hear the tower bell;
They do not know the hunger, they do not hear the cry,
Make way for German labour, clear the road for us!

Hurrah for German labour, the red flag in the front,
The swastika must triumph, surrounded by the light of freedom.
German men are fighting for a new era,
We will not rest, nor will we stop, until Germany is liberated.

This song of the "*Wiener Jungarbeiter*" shows that the German workers in Austria know the same need and the same longing as their fellow workers in Germany, that they strive for the Greater German Reich under the swastika despite all the oppression. In 1928, Horst Wessel had been making inquiries among the Viennese workers. He, the student, also sought the national community there, and went among the people, to meetings of both friends and opponents, wanting to hear what they thought. Only then could he know what to say to them, how to help them. He brought a lot of experience with him to Berlin. One evening, twenty of them sat close to the lectern during a large SPD meeting in the north of Berlin. One of the very great leaders over there was talking about the fulfillment policy towards the enemies of the World War. They should be content and bow down, then the workers of the enemy countries would help them fraternally, then foreign countries would continue to lend them money; with this they could then govern and carry out great projects. He went on to speak of the collective conscience and of the general brotherhood of peoples, calling it the *Internationale*. When he said this, there was a strong roar of applause and clapping of hands.

Another speaker appeared: a non-native, who had a lot to say about the German schoolchildren in Greater Berlin. He called on the parents to take their children out of religious education and send them to secular schools, because there was no God; the churches should be turned into movie theatres and trade union halls. And the next Saturday they should all send their children with red flags; there would be a freethinkers' meeting and afterwards a parade of children through the city, and so it went on for a while. They all listened devoutly and were outraged when heckles came from among the twenty guests. And suddenly Horst Wessel stood up at the lectern. "I may still be very young," he began, "but you see, it is precisely the innocent youth who ultimately suffer the most from today's state of affairs." Then he passionately lashed out at the first speaker: "German community members, you let your leaders lead you around by the nose! Since the dictate of Versailles you have been squeezed dry by foreign countries, and your leaders still persuade you to give more. It is the worker who suffers most. The borrowed money is a swindle, which makes you even poorer, because you have to pay it back with high interest. Your party wanted to smash capitalism, but capitalism has never flourished in the world as it does now. And has the collective conscience ever helped you? Let all strife be; come together in the national community and help yourselves. Come to Adolf Hitler; he makes one people out of all. With us every one is a German worker, whether he works with his head or with his hands. We know no class arrogance and no class hatred, but only honest, working German community members. Heil Hitler!" Most of them shouted furiously, but a few thought: *I'll go to a Nazi meeting next time; I have to hear more.*

Another time, there was a communist meeting in the Pharus meeting hall. There was a speaker at the lectern: "Comrades, you workers are a class of your own, you alone must have power in the state, like in Russia; you must always hate and beat to death the others, the rich, the bourgeois, and the farmers! Away with the vermin! Then we too will have paradise like in Russia; then you will have food and water and a wonderful life! Long live the civil war, long live Soviet Russia!" Again Horst Wessel stood up and spoke to the flood of hatred and shouting: "Yes, your workers' paradise! One of you has come back from Russia; let me tell you about him! Hard work in the mines, always under supervision. Miserable wages and miserable food, miserable wooden barracks in the winter! A strike? Yes, that's what you're telling the others about. That doesn't happen in your workers' paradise; they throw someone like that in jail or shoot them!" A raucous roar rumbled over him, but he made himself heard. "Do you know where your comrade is now? He has recognized your deception; he is in the only true national community, where there is no class hatred. He is with us; he is in my storm! Down there he sits with our people! Heil Hitler!" All hell broke loose! A scuffle! Bleeding, they fought their way through and gathered a few streets away. What's that? There are three strangers with them? Informers? "We want to come to you; your speaker is right about Russia. Yesterday my brother came back; he told us. He's now in the hospital in misery. He's coming to you too!"

There was a lot of fun at a meeting of the Economic Party. A fat master baker had just been elected chairman and gave a speech. He said that he would ask the government to reduce the working hours of bakers, because they had a harder job than the others. A master locksmith spoke out against this, and the meeting threatened to degenerate into a dispute between the professions. Then from one corner came a shout: "German unity! Germany, awake!" Some hurriedly searched for their coats and hats and headed for the exit. Nazis have entered the hall! But that's what the association papers are supposed to say, that the Nazis want to blow up their meeting! And again Horst Wessel spoke with passion as well as mockery. He castigated the selfish aims of the individual professions, where everyone wants to earn a lot and work little, without regard for the national welfare. He showed them the new goal of work: "Common interest comes before self-interest!" He showed them the national community of National Socialism, where everyone is to serve the state according to his or her abilities. In this way he spoke and campaigned in meetings of others and in his own for the soul of each individual, for the new state which is to give work and bread to all community members. Second only to Dr. Goebbels, he became the most active speaker in Berlin, but he also became the most hated SA man. The communists had to witness Horst Wessel seizing their best people and pulling them over to him, turning deceived communists into German community members. "Down with the dog! We'll have to beat him to a pulp!" was soon the slogan with them. One morning, as Horst was leaving the house in the Jüdenstraße with his brother, he saw a swastika painted on the front door, and behind it three skulls and crossbones; below them, scribbled in red chalk, was a sickle and hammer, the sign of the communists. "Horst, this is for you," says Werner, "the communists are sending you their greetings. Watch out!" "Oh, take if off; wipe it away so that the mother doesn't see it!" Even more often after that there was such a sign on the front door. Horst Wessel was not intimidated. He went further out among the people, and often went alone to pubs where communists were also present, sat down at the table with them, and talked back and forth. Despite their hatred of him, they respected him, and one of the leaders over there suggested that he leave Berlin or come over to them. Where did Horst get the strength for this fight against the red terror, against an infested Berlin? It was his passionate belief in Adolf Hitler and his mission to create a great German national community out of the parties, out of southern and northern Germans, out of Protestants and Catholics, out of citizens, farmers, and workers.

THE *STURMFÜHRER*

Wir tragen an unserm braunen Kleid
Die Sturmnummer 5 am Kragen.
Und wenn es gilt, sind wir stets bereit,
Für Deutschland das Leben zu wagen.
Ja, wir sind Nationalsozialisten genannt,
Als 5. Sturmabteilung bekannt.

Ob Ausmarsch oder Versammlungsschlacht,
Wir müssen es immer beweisen.
Ob vor uns die Schupopistole kracht,
Ob die Luft Voller Steine und Eisen,
Ja, in jedem Falle geht Mann für Mann
Vom 5. Sturm an den Feind heran.

Für uns da gibt es kein Hindernis,
Vor uns da muß alles weichen.
Wo wir angreifen, da ist es gewiß,
Daß die Unsern den Sieg erreichen.
Wo andere greifen vergeblich an,
Da zieht man den 5. Sturm heran.

We wear on our brown shirt
The storm number 5 on our collar.
And when it's time, we're always ready,
To risk our lives for Germany.
Yes, we are called National Socialists,
Known as the 5th Sturmabteilung.

Whether marching out or fighting at rallies,
We must always prove ourselves.
Whether the *Schupo* pistol bangs in front of us,
Whether the air is full of stones and iron,
Yes, in every case, man for man
From the 5th Storm towards the enemy.

For us there is no obstacle,
Before us all must give way.
Where we attack, there it is certain,
That ours will achieve victory.
Where others attack in vain,
There we bring in the 5th Storm.

Storm 5 sang its storm hymn with roaring voices. In marching columns of three they returned from a publicity march. In front was the flag and *Sturmführer* Horst Wessel; there had been bloodshed again, for in the middle of the worst district of Berlin, in the east at Friedrichshain, Storm 5 had taken up residence, in the middle of a district that had hitherto been the undisputed territory of the communists, in which Soviet flags hung from every house. It was an insult to the Nazis—and again it was this fellow, Horst Wessel, who sat down in their midst!

They reached the storm pub at Friedrichshain. "Halt! Dismissed!" sounded the command, and everyone hurried into the storm pub. "He's quite a guy, Horst! How annoyed they were outside about his new song! But that also fits in with Storm 5!" It had only been a little over a month since Horst Wessel wore the three stars of the *Sturmführer* on his left shoulder. What good posts he had been offered, including the *Sturmführer* post in his old Second Storm, where everyone knew and loved him, where he could rely on everyone! He refused everything and asked for the small *Truppführer* post of Troop 34 in the middle of the red east. His comrades didn't understand him. "Horst, leave it be; it's a lost cause, you'll be ruined," they said, "and your new squad, those ten men, they have no say in the matter—even if they can swear like pirates!" Nothing had helped. On May 1st, 1929, he took over that nasty lot. He saw himself standing in front of them that first evening, he, the young student, in front of mostly veteran soldiers and former *Freikorps* members. He had to be sharp. On the one hand he whistled at them like recruits, then again he sat with them at the storm evening meetings, sang and drank with them, soon knew their good and bad sides, was always together with them in other ways too, and honed and educated them and—they submitted, they felt in him both a comrade and a leader. Yes, those storm evening meetings! He attracted new people like a magnet; after a month he already had more than a hundred who stuck together in the middle of the communist quarter through thick and thin. Berlin's top SA leader turned the group into an independent storm: the dreaded Storm 5, the Horst Wessel Storm. Those storm evening meetings under Horst Wessel! Everyone looked forward to them; they forgot how dirty they were, they sat together with all those who thought the same way. It was a community with a heartbeat; without this SA comradeship, life was nothing! And all the things they took with them on those evenings! Horst's wonderful storm hymns were sung. How simply and grippingly he could show them what they were fighting, starving, and bleeding for. The way they sat together there without class distinction and without class hatred, the student next to the brewer, the worker next to the young merchant, the gray-haired office worker next to the construction student: they were a national community on a small scale, and that's how it should be in the great German fatherland. He impressed upon them again and again that the SA man was the bearer of the National Socialist revolution, that everything great and new was only achieved through blood and sacrifice. So he hammered them hard, so he sang to them again and again the proud song of the SA man, the most loyal fighter of Adolf Hitler. Once he wanted to explain to them why voting under National Socialism was not based on majority decisions; he wanted to explain to them the meaning of the idea of the Führer, when one of them shouted, "Horst, leave it, we know what a Führer is; we only have to look at you!" There the SA spirit grew, there a bond for life and death was formed. It was true, the song: "Where others attack in vain, there you call in Storm 5!" "Down with the red street terror!" That was the slogan. Out with the stock market swindlers and racketeers from Germany!

What a great thing had occurred shortly thereafter. A communist terrorist bar, which was terrorizing the whole area, was unceremoniously occupied and the landlord and the communist groups inside were so intimidated and ridiculed that the red terror in the area was broken. On that occasion, Storm 5 was returning from a training exercise in the countryside. Then Horst Wessel had the idea of driving his trucks through the completely Bolshevik Fischerkietz in the old town for the first time. The *Sturmführer* could rely on his men! The cars roared up; the swastika flag rattled on the one in front. The storm hymns resounded and chants rang out: "Down with the red terror! Germany, awake!" Advertising leaflets fluttered down. The residents were stunned by this insolence. Then the red mob came rushing out of all the houses and surrounded the trucks. Up there they stood, the men of Storm 5, with determined faces, shoulder straps in hand, ready to hurl themselves into the frying pan at the command of the *Sturmführer*. What was that? Instead of making a move to get out of there, the foremost car stopped. Horst Wessel climbed up on the deck and spoke to the people, who now, stunned by so much audacity, stopped their shouting and listened. "We warn you for the last time about attacking individual National Socialists here in the Fischerkietz. The German streets belong to the German fighters of Adolf Hitler and not to the red gangs of Moscow. Down with the murderous communists! Heil Hitler!" Cheeringly, the salute to the Führer rang out for the first time from a closed SA formation in this disreputable part of the city. Slowly the cars drove through the raging crowd. Paralyzed by the sudden break-in of the Nazis, the overwhelming force dared not attack; the breach into the closed Red Front succeeded there. How proud Storm 5 was of its dashing *Sturmführer*, who took one red stronghold after another! How this pride grew into jubilation when it came out that Horst had persuaded the supreme SA leader of Berlin to allow his storm to lead a shawm band. Shawms! That had only existed with the communists before. What a rage there was when, for the first time, Storm 5 marched through the streets to the tantalizing sounds of its own shawm band! Hatred rose like a wall against this daring *Sturmführer*. He again found the skull and crossbones painted on his front door, but the bond of love and loyalty of Storm 5 wrapped itself ever-more tightly around its *Sturmführer* Horst Wessel! Every single one of them was bound to him in life and death; there was real leadership and real loyalty.

PARTY CONGRESS IN NUREMBERG 1929

Die Fahne hoch! Die Reihen dicht geschlossen.
SA. marschiert mit ruhig festem Schritt.

Kam'raden, die Rotfront und Reaktion erschossen,
Marschier'n im Geist in unsern Reihen mit. (x2)

Die Straße frei den braunen Bataillonen,
Die Straße frei dem Sturmabteilungsmann!

Es schaun auf's Hakenkreuz voll Hoffnung schon Millionen,
Der Tag für Freiheit und für Brot bricht an. (x2)

Zum letztenmal wird nun Appell geblasen,
Zum Kampfe steh'n wir alle schon bereit.

Bald flattern Hitlerfahnen über allen Straßen.
Die Knechtschaft dauert nur noch kurze Zeit! (x2)

Die Fahne hoch! Die Reihen dicht geschlossen.
SA. marschiert mit ruhig festem Schritt.

Kam'raden, die Rotfront und Reaktion erschossen,
Marschier'n im Geist in unsern Reihen mit. (x2)
Raise the flag! The ranks tightly closed!
The SA marches with calm, steady step.

Comrades shot by Red Front and reactionaries
March in spirit within our ranks. (x2)

Clear the streets for the brown battalions,
Clear the streets for the Sturmabteilung man!

Millions are looking upon the swastikas full of hope,
The day of freedom and of bread dawns! (x2)

For the last time, the call to arms resounds!
For the fight, we all stand prepared!

Already Hitler's banners fly over all the streets.
The time of bondage will last but a little while now! (x2)

Raise the flag! The ranks tightly closed!
The SA marches with calm, steady step.

Comrades shot by Red Front and reactionaries
March in spirit within our ranks. (x2)

Storm 5 sings its new victorious storm hymn in Nuremberg, marching in an endless line from the railway station through the city. The population, crowded around the streets, listens. Who is this storm with the victoriously smiling young *Sturmführer* at its head? What is this rhythm and what are these words? They push their way in, joining the strange storm. They hear of dead comrades marching along in spirit in the brown ranks. They hear what they have felt for a long time, what they long for from the bottom of their hearts. The young voices of the brown fighters with the 5 on their collars call out to them: "*Es schaun aufs Hakenkreuz voll Hoffnung schon Millionen; der Tag für Freiheit und für Brot bricht an!*"[44] Yes, the hope of a turnaround in Germany's misery is promised to them by this striking song. They will be free from dark despair; life will have a purpose again. Powerfully they are seized by the melody and the sweeping words of this song. Their eyes shining, they look at the long procession of storm banners and hear the storm chant: "*Bald flattern Hitlerfahnen über allen Straßen; die Knechtschaft dauert nur noch kurze Zeit!*"[45] This is the awakened young Germany singing here, cheering defiance and victory in the immortal words of the "Horst Wessel Song": "*Die Fahne Hoch!*"

---

[44] Millions are already looking at the swastika, full of hope; the day for freedom and for bread is dawning!
[45] Soon Hitler-flags will flutter over all streets; slavery will only last a short time!

The young *Sturmführer* thought back with a smile to the preparations made in Berlin for the party congress. At the storm evening meetings, he had told his comrades about the 1927 party congress he had attended, about the leader Adolf Hitler, about his compelling words, about the victorious confidence in his eyes. They all wanted to come along, provided they weren't lying in hospitals with wounds. They had saved up and given up cigarettes in order to raise the money for the trip. Finally, on August 2nd, the time had come. First, roll call at the Jüdenhof, then marching off with luggage to the Anhalter railway station: a jolly journey in packed crowds. Next, arrival in Nuremberg and the first great joy: the Führer stood in the station hall to greet all his supporters. Then the entry into the city, cheering crowds, the mood of victory on everyone's face, and then the attention, the shining eyes all around when his song rang out: *"Die Fahne Hoch!"*

In the evening there was a torchlit procession, the streets were packed with people, with an unmistakable procession of brown torchbearers in the middle. There were no opponents anywhere, nor were there the calls of "Red Front!"—just a festively dressed, enthusiastic crowd. Could this really be? They, who were mocked, pelted with stones, and shot down, were celebrated and honored here? So the movement in the Reich grew and took hold of the people. Germany awoke and the SA marched into the future, confident of victory. What were the battles in Berlin, what was injury and death in the face of this glorious advance of National Socialism! They passed the Führer, who kept raising his hand in greeting. They, Hitler's soldiers from all over the Reich, were seized by a frenzy of joy; glowing torchlight, singing, music, and salutes to the Führer enveloped them. Horst Wessel felt that this was the high point, the apex of his young life. It must have been the same in those August days of 1914, when the field-gray soldiers marched through the streets accompanied by the cheers of the people, with flowers and music. Back then, too, it was a national community that went into battle. No one thought of death, not then and not now. Horst thought of the student regiments of Langemark, of their sacrificial death with the *"Deutschlandlied"* on their lips. The highest thing was to lay down one's life for a great cause; to die defiantly and defensively, as he had so often told his comrades at the storm evening meetings. In the glowing jubilation of that August day in 1929, he vowed anew to fight for Germany's salvation, and if necessary to die like those at Langemark, those doomed to die.

Leader duties woke him from his thoughts. He had to take his men to their quarters late at night. Finally everyone fell asleep. What was that? A sudden alarm! "Get ready! Raid on small squads of our people!" So up from the compound, out into the night! Those cowards, hiding from the SA during the day! They didn't get much sleep that night. Early in the morning they marched to Luitpoldhain. Sixty thousand of Adolf Hitler's soldiers were gathered in front of their supreme leader, a proud image of the German liberation army. In the midst of them was the Berlin Storm 5 with its young *Sturmführer* Horst Wessel. Hearts beat high in unison with the tens of thousands facing the Führer. And then Hitler spoke to his SA, committing them anew to the holy fight for Germany. Storm flags were consecrated by him; the fallen were remembered in loyal solidarity. The procession followed. Cheers, singing, and flowers upon flowers as Hitler's guard marched through the crowded streets. Then it was time to say goodbye to Nuremberg and head off to battle! A song from the Great War, taught him by his father, came to Horst Wessel's mind as he said goodbye to all the faithful from Nuremberg: *"Ein Tag der Rosen im August, da hat die Garde fortgemußt."* [46]

So Adolf Hitler's guards also went forth from the jubilation of the August days into storm and battle.

---

[46] "A Day of Roses in August, the guards had to leave." These two verses are also the name of a German silent film from 1927. The film takes place in August 1914 at the beginning of the First World War. It is about the start of WWI when the German soldiers were preparing to leave for battle.

STRUGGLE AND SORROW

Brüder in Zechen und Gruben,
Brüder ihr hinter dem Pflug,
Aus den Fabriken und Stuben
Folgt unseres Banners Zug.

Börsengauner und Schieber
Knechten das Vaterland;
Wir wollen ehrlich verdienen,
Fleißig mit schaffender Hand.

Hitler ist unser Führer,
Ihn lohnt nicht gold'ner Sold,
Der von den jüdischen Thronen
Vor seine Füße rollt.

Einst kommt der Tag der Rache,
Einmal, da werden wir frei,
Schaffendes Deutschland erwache,
Brich deine Ketten entzwei.

Dann laßt das Banner fliegen,
Daß unsere Feinde es seh'n,
Immer werden wir siegen,
Wenn wir zusammen steh'n.

Hitler treu ergeben,
Treu bis in den Tod.
Hitler wird uns führen
Einst aus dieser Not.

Brothers in mines and coal pits,
Brothers behind the plough,
From factories and taverns
Follow our banner's march.

Swindlers and racketeers
Subjugate the fatherland;
We want to earn honestly
With an industrious, working hand.

Hitler is our leader,
He is not paid in gold,
That from the Jewish thrones
Rolls before his feet.

One day revenge will come,
One day we shall be free,
Awake, creative Germany,
Break your chains.

Then let the banner wave
So that our enemies may see,
We will always be victorious
If we stand together

Loyal to Hitler,
Loyal to the death
Hitler will lead us
Out of this misery one day.

The struggle for the soul of the people, the national community that was emerging, and the struggle for the soul of the individual community member—the Führer in Nuremberg had repeatedly hammered all this into their heads as a goal. Horst Wessel was a student; most of the comrades in his storm were workers. He got along with them; they had already been won over and they were of the same spirit as him. But how could he get close to the many agitated workers outside? He understood them and could talk to them, but when did he have enough opportunity? Only in passing or in meetings. He had to get to know their work, to be with them all the time, to show them that they were not a despised class that had to take revenge for being held in contempt by others by hating everyone else as a class. So he decided to become a worker, to be their equal, to show them that there was no need for a gap between those working with their hands and those working with their heads, and that every job had its value and its honor.

First he became a taxi driver. There were often discussions among his colleagues when their cars were parked in a long line. He was the only Nazi; the others were communists, SPD, or Reichsbanner. They agreed immediately when the conversation turned to the fat racketeers they often had to drive. "The other day I was driving this guy," Horst's colleague Anton recounted. "He had a little grocery shop next to us on the Kösliner Straße a year and a half ago; he knows me very well. Now he looks over me, shouts, 'Driver, drive me to the stock exchange!' throws a three-mark piece on my seat, and walks away. To him we are dirt!"

Then the conversation turned to the capitalists. "They live off us proletarians," shouted one, "and what is worse, they give Hitler and the Nazis their money so that they can subjugate the workers. Here it is again in *Die Rote Fahne*, how uniformed Nazi bandits attacked class-conscious workers. You're one of those, too," he said to Horst. "Who pays for your uniforms if not the capitalists?"—This is where the work of enlightening the enraged and misguided community members began; after all, they read nothing but the lying reports of *Die Rote Fahne* and the *Vorwärts*. How were they to know that every SA man saved up for his uniform by himself, that he hates capitalism, that he wants to unite all honest workers in a national and social national community? "Fight for the soul of the individual community member!" the Führer had said.

Horst Wessel continued to fight; the glory of the days of Nuremberg gave him strength and showed him the way. "Mother," he said one day, "don't be angry with me; I have to leave you. I have rented a room in the Frankfurter Straße; I have become a laborer, an excavator, and I want to live like them. I want to get to know them completely. I'll come to you often, as soon as I have time!" His mother could not stop him. So he became a shipper in the construction of the underground railway.[47] His back hurt, he could hardly lift his arms, and his hands got blisters and calluses, but he held on. First the other workers gave him sideways looks, then they accepted him as one of their own and opened their hearts to him. It was always the same with them: either they were incited to class hatred by the red heresies, or they plodded along indifferently and dully from the workplace to the pub and from there to the bedroom. Here Horst Wessel sowed the new seeds of the national community; from there he took some of them to his storm evening meetings, restored their faith in the value and honor of work, and turned them into Adolf Hitler's most loyal fighters.

Soon his storm had grown to two hundred and fifty men. Then a new thought occurred to him. In front of the labor offices, on the stairs, in the corridors of the unemployment offices, there was red terror; no Nazi could dare say a word, because if the reds recognized him, he would get a beating. Horst Wessel drew up plans for the whole of Berlin, discussed them with Dr. Goebbels, and then the fight for the unemployment offices began. The communists fought back with pistol and brass knuckles, but the SA prevailed. Thus, bit by bit, the influence of the reds in Greater Berlin was broken. Word soon spread about who had been the originator of the plan. Poisonous hatred swelled against the Nazi dog, the damned Horst Wessel. To hell with his national community; that was nothing for the red leaders, for they could only live and profit from class hatred and class struggle. To hell above all with the dangerous Horst Wessel!

Fate, which had so far shone victoriously for him in the struggle for his people, also sent him darkness after the great light. On December 23rd, Horst Wessel and his Storm 5 stood at the open grave of the murdered SA comrade Fischer and lowered the storm flag over his coffin. At the same time, high up in the Giant Mountains, his brother Werner died a snowy death. He had gone up with the Berlin National Socialist ski group and died with three others in a blizzard. Horst brought his dead brother to Berlin in a truck. Then Werner was laid out in the vicarage in the Jüdenstraße. Comrades of Storm 1 held the wake on both sides of the coffin. December 28th approached; mother, brother, and sister had to say goodbye to the

---

[47] It is not immediately apparent why Wessel is referred to both as an excavator and a shipper, but we could guess that he is moving the dirt, perhaps by driving a truck— thus an excavator as well as a shipper.

dear deceased. The *Sturmführer* of Werner's standard carried the coffin down. In the old cemetery of St. Nikolai, they laid Werner next to his father. As a last greeting, thousands of the SA sang the dead man's song:

> *Du kleiner Tambur, schlage ein,*
> *Kameraden, laßt die Banner wehen.*
> *Wir woll'n nicht länger Knechte sein,*
> *Alldeutschland sieht ein Auferstehen!*
> *Lebwohl, lebwohl, du stolze Zier,*
> *Du Sturmsoldat von der Standarte vier!*

> You little drummer, play a tune,
> Comrades, let the banners wave,
> We no longer want to be slaves
> All of Germany will rise again!
> Farewell, farewell, you proud jewel,
> You Stormtrooper of Standard 4!

Deeply moved, Horst was the last to remain at his brother's grave to say goodbye.

The year 1930 began badly. One day, his comrades discovered him in his apartment with the communist widow Salm, sitting on the sofa and staring ahead, uttering muddled words. They brought him home to his mother with a severe fever. There he lay on the verge of death, fantasizing that he was to blame for Werner's death, that Werner would catch up with him this year. Those were frightening days for mother and sister; were they now to lose Horst too? At last there was a slight improvement, and then things got better quickly. He had the will to get well. At last the time had come. He just wanted to get his things from the Große Frankfurter Straße, then he was to go away and recover. Everything would still be all right.

ROTMORD

Von all unsern Kameraden	Of all the comrades,
War keiner so lieb und so gut	None was as kind and as good
Als unser Sturmführer Wessel,	As our *Sturmführer* Wessel,
Ein lustiges Hakenkreuzblut.	A jolly swastika blood.
Wir saßen so fröhlich beisammen	We sat together so happily
In mancher so stürmischen Nacht.	On a stormy night,
Mit seinen Hitlerliedern	With his Hitler songs
Hat er uns so fröhlich gemacht.	He made us so happy.
Da kam eine feindliche Kugel	Then came an enemy bullet
Von roter Mordbubenhand.	From a red murderer's hand.
Horst Wessel, du ließest dein Leben	Horst Wessel, you gave your life
Für Hitler und Vaterland.[48]	For Hitler and Fatherland!

Horst Wessel entered his apartment in the late afternoon of January 14th, 1930. His landlady, the communist widow Salm, was sneaking around him. *What, so the guy didn't die after all? Is he here again? I'll give him a drink!*—Quickly down the stairs; she knows where to find her people. In the Dragonerstraße, in the Bär tavern, they were sitting together, playing cards. Suddenly the woman stood among them. "That dog, Wessel, is back! Go! Now is the time; now you can kill him!" They threw down their cards and listened. That Wessel, the dangerous Nazi dog, the "terror of the East," who had ruined everything for them? He had been tempting fate for far too long! First the shawm band, then the insolent parades through the red districts. And the other day the provocative funeral of the other Wessel, what damage did all that do to the red reputation! But the worst thing was that on the day of the funeral one of their leaders was killed; no matter

---

[48] This song can be sung to the melody of "*Wenn alle Untreu Werden.*"

who did it, the brown bandits are to blame! And Wessel, he's going to get it now! Or should we wait and ask Kupferstein, the Soviet leader, in the Karl Liebknecht House first? "What, you want to be Red Front?" cried Else Cohn, an ugly anti-fascist girl. "You want to let the dog get away, you cowards?" Wessel is a dangerous fellow! The widow Salm was quickly sent to the Galsk pub on the Mulackstraße to get reinforcements. She brought the right people with her. Ali Höhler, just back from prison, was the ringleader. Sixteen men snuck into the Große Frankfurter Straße, snuck up the stairs, and lay in wait. They sent the widow Salm up. Maybe there are more Nazi dogs with him? She sent word: only two women are there, helping to pack. Quick, he'll be ready in a minute. Quietly she opened the corridor door to the murder-gang.

Horst Wessel was sitting upstairs. He had paused in the middle of packing. Depart? Abandon his storm? Wasn't that desertion? He saw the shining storm flags in front of him in Nuremberg, heard the Führer speak. The glow of the days of Nuremberg lifted him above all doubts. His health? His mother? Honor and duty bound him; he was a fighter for Adolf Hitler. He stayed there; he wanted to fight on over red Berlin!

There was a knock. It must have been Fiedler and Sprengel, the SA comrades. He wanted to tell them straight away that he was staying. "Come in, Albert," he called and opened the door. There was Rotmord standing outside. Shots were fired. Hit several times in the mouth, Horst Wessel was rolling in his blood. With raw jeers, the gang slunk away. "He's finished, the Nazi dog!"

The women tried to stop the bleeding; one of them ran to the storm pub across the street. They didn't want to believe it. They came and saw him lying; they took him to the hospital at Friedrichshain. He was operated on, but there was little hope. His mother and sister Inge were allowed to see him from a distance. From his thickly bandaged head, Horst's eyes shone comfortingly at them.

In pavilion 7, the *Sturmführer* of Storm 5 lay struggling with death. Then the hot will to live won out, the bullets could be removed, and the wounds began to heal. Mother and sister sat at his bedside: my God, just don't lose Horst too! Dr. Goebbels came; the people of his storm were allowed to pass by the open door and saluted their *Sturmführer* with the Hitler-salute. Later they were allowed to sit at his bedside for a short time: locksmiths, students, workers, the

Hohenzollern Prince August Wilhelm: all fighters for Adolf Hitler, and the same love and hope shone from their eyes.

Once again the red murder-beast made an attempt. It wanted to throw hand grenades into pavilion 7. The vigilance of the SA beat the dehumanized horde out. Mother and sister received threatening letters; the SA also protected the house in the Jüdenstraße.

Then came the end. Blood poisoning took away Horst's strength. All the doctors' efforts were in vain. Dr. Goebbels sat with him. Wrestling with death, Horst Wessel looked ahead to the victory of the freedom movement. On Sunday February 23rd at half past seven in the morning, he died in the arms of his mother and sister and entered the brown storm of the martyrs of National Socialism.

LOWER THE FLAGS

Schwarz ist das Kreuz und weiß ist das Feld,
Rot ist das Tuch, das der Fähnrich hält.
Braune Soldaten, die stürmen, stürmen, stürmen durch die Nacht,
Kämpfen für Deutschland und halten treue Wacht.

Kampf ist das Schicksal, das Gott uns gab,
Drum schreckt uns auch nicht das kühle Grab.
Braune Soldaten, die stürmen, stürmen, stürmen, durch die Nacht,
Kämpfen für Deutschlands und halten treue Wacht.

Sollt' ich dann sterben auf blutigem Feld,
Haltet die Fahne, vom Kampfruf umgellt.
Braune Soldaten, die stürmen, stürmen, stürmen durch die Nacht,
Kämpfen für Deutschland und halten treue Wacht.

Braun ist die Erde, in die ihr mich legt,
Braun ist die Sturmflut, die Deutschland durchfegt.
Braune Soldaten, die stürmen, stürmen, stürmen durch die Nacht,
Kämpfen für Deutschland und halten treue Wacht.

Kommt ihr nach Hause und frei ist das Land,
Dann gebt uns Toten die Fahn' in die Hand,
Tote Soldaten, die stehen, stehen, stehen in der Nacht,
Halten für Deutschland auf immer treue Wacht.

Black is the cross and white is the patch,
Red is the cloth that the standard-bearer holds.
Brown soldiers, storming, storming, storming through the night,
Fight for Germany and keep faithful watch.

Struggle is the destiny God gave us,
Therefore even the cold grave does not frighten us.
Brown soldiers, storming, storming, storming through the night,
Fight for Germany and keep faithful watch.

Should I then die on a bloody field,
Hold the flag, surrounded by the battle cry.
Brown soldiers, storming, storming, storming through the night,
Fight for Germany and keep faithful watch.

Brown is the earth in which you put me,
Brown is the storm tide that sweeps through Germany.
Brown soldiers, storming, storming, storming through the night,
Fight for Germany and keep faithful watch.

When you come home and the land is free,
Then put the flag in the hands of us dead,
Dead soldiers, standing, standing, standing in the night,
Keep faithful watch over Germany forever.

Storm 5 fetched its dead *Sturmführer* and brought him home to his mother. Horst Wessel was solemnly laid out in the room where his brother had lain two months ago. Around him were laurel leaves, flowers, burning candles, the storm flags of the standard, in the middle his flag of Storm 5, and to the right and left of it the two flags of the Normannia and Alemannia Corps. On both sides of the coffin, the comrades of the SA and fellow Corps members stood vigil, unmoving, with weeping hearts and burning eyes. Flowers and wreaths were there from all over Germany, as well as letters to the mother and the sister. SA comrades had written from the prisons. All the good people in the country were awakened by the sacrificial death of this young hero. People flocked from near and far to see the dead man and to pledge eternal loyalty to the freedom movement at his coffin. A dignified funeral was to be prepared, worthy of the sacrifices made by the dead *Sturmführer*. German youth, men, and women wanted to show how they honored German freedom fighters. But the police, especially Mr. Zörgiebel, forbade everything. One had to be considerate of the mood of the red population, had to not irritate them, so they said. Only a very small funeral, no swastika flags—just don't attract attention! So Inge Wessel made the difficult pilgrimage for her dead brother. She was sent away from the police headquarters with empty words. In the pouring rain she went to the Reich President's Palace. Hindenburg, yes, Hindenburg, her father's friend, would help her. She only got as far as the State Secretary. They were very sorry, very polite, but wouldn't let her through to Hindenburg. Again to Zörgiebel. It remained the same: only seven closed funeral cars were to follow the coffin. All other escorts were forbidden. The usual phrases: consideration, danger of civil war. At the cemetery itself, the other mourners could be present.

March 1st approached: the last journey of the dead fighter for Germany. Arm-in-arm, mother and daughter stood before the dead man for the last time; it was time to say goodbye again. "First Werner," sobbed the mother, "and now Horst, my dear, dear boy."

The coffin had closed, it was wrapped in a large swastika flag, and the two Corps caps and Horst's SA cap lay on top. The *Sturmführer* approached the coffin. Bad things happened then. Police entered, demanded the removal of the German freedom flag, and fierce words were spoken. The coffin was finally surrounded with wreaths and flowers so that the flag could not be seen.

The procession started to move. The brown uniforms were missing, but the blue uniforms of the *Schupo* men were there, who had to protect the last path of a German freedom fighter in the capital of the German Reich with a rubber truncheon. What happened then is to be burned as a disgrace into the hearts of German youth forever, is to kindle their eternal hatred against everything base and un-German that ever dares to raise its head again. Rotmord knew no respect or reverence even for the dead. Suddenly there was wild shouting, stones hurled at the hearse, shots, and scuffles. The red mob rushed forward to overturn the wagon. The police machine guns rattled against Rotmord; they had to protect a dead man from living beasts. In front of the Nikolai cemetery, which was densely occupied by SA, a new furious attack began. Many an SA man sank wounded to the ground. Finally the cemetery was reached. SA, Stahlhelm, and student associations formed a line. The wreaths fell from the coffin. There they were finally allowed to show the swastika flag. *Sturmführer* Horst Wessel was lowered into the tomb between his father and brother. Once again the red disgrace outside raised howls and roars with stones flying over the cemetery wall until the police chased them back. The students gave the dead Corps brother a ribbon and cap to take to his grave; Captain Göring threw Horst's storm cap into the tomb, and the priest spoke. Then the song, Horst Wessel's song, the song of the SA, "*Die Fahne Hoch*" rang out over the old cemetery; it was like an oath of the thousands to become like the young hero, to fight forever, forever for Germany. Then Dr. Goebbels spoke and he spoke to the dead man as if he was still alive, still standing before him:

"And then when the SA is assembled for the big roll call, when each individual is called, then the Führer will also call your name, Comrade Wessel! And all, all the SA men will answer as if from one mouth: 'here!'—for the SA—that is Horst Wessel!" Quietly he continued, "Here stands a German woman, stands the mother of Werner and Horst Wessel. Two splendid sons she once had, now both rest in their graves. No man on earth can comfort you, mother, but know this: your sons are all of us! Storms will march, brown storms, endlessly, endlessly. The drums rumble, the whistles cheer, the swastika flags wave brightly over all the streets. One of them is there, his hand on his belt, the storm strap under his chin—he marches along, a young laugh on his red lips and in his bright eyes. It may be this one or that one—no one knows him, perhaps, and yet everyone senses him. Once he was a wanderer between two worlds, between yesterday and tomorrow, between what was and what is to come. He was a fighter for the awakening Germany, for freedom and bread; he was a young hero—and will always be to us what he was, to us and soon to the whole great Fatherland: a young, radiant hero! Wherever Germany is, there you are too, Horst Wessel. Soon, soon, our flags will bend low over you, my young comrade, and over the flag cloth that wraps you. But then it will be as if you shouted the words you taught us, the proud words: 'raise the flags!' And the flags will rise again, as you will, from death towards a warm life—and with them your spirit will rise from the tomb, will penetrate deep into our hearts, will live in us for all time, as long as we are allowed to breathe!"

IMMORTALITY

Das Hakenkreuz

Das Hakenkreuz im weißen Feld
Auf feuerrotem Grunde
Gibt frei und offen aller Welt
Die hochgemute Kunde:
Wer sich um dieses Zeichen schart,
Ist deutsch mit Seele, Sinn und Art,
Und nicht bloß mit dem Munde.

Das Hakenkreuz im weißen Feld
Auf feuerrotem Grunde
Zum Volksmal ward es auserwählt
In ernster Schicksalsstunde,
Als unter Schmerzen, heiß und tief,
Das Vaterland um Hilfe rief,
Dass teure, Todeswunde.

Das Hakenkreuz im weißen Feld
Auf feuerrotem Grunde
Hat uns mit stolzem Mut beseelt;
Es schlägt in unserer Runde
Kein Herz, das feig' die Treue bricht.
Wir fürchten Tod und Teufel nicht!
Mit uns ist Gott im Bunde.

The Swastika

The swastika in the white patch
On a fiery red background
Gives freely and openly to all the world
The proud message:
Whoever rallies around this sign
Is German in soul, mind, and manner,
And not merely in his words.

The swastika in the white patch
On a fiery red background
It was chosen as a national symbol
In a serious hour of destiny,
When in pain, passionate and intense,
The fatherland called for help,
The costly, fatal wound.

The swastika in the white patch
On a fiery red background
Has inspired us with proud courage;
There beats in our midst
No heart that cowardly breaks loyalty.
We do not fear death and the devil!
God is in alliance with us.

Horst Wessel, you *Sturmführer*! You foresaw prophetically the victory of the swastika. You had to die to become a wake-up call for many lost and indifferent people; you had to die to show German youth the way, the way to the new Germany, which can only arise through blood and sacrifice, through discipline and loyalty. You could not live to see the day of victory: January 30th, 1933, when your storm and tens of thousands of SA comrades marched past in your Berlin, marched under blazing torches past the grasping field marshal of the World War and your leader Adolf Hitler, the chancellor of the German Reich, no longer despised and persecuted, but as the victors and saviors of the new Germany. You have passed away, you have become the *Sturmführer* of the brown storm of the dead up there, and yet you live among us as an immortal. Your old storm, grown mightily, marches today behind the proud standard that bears the name "Horst Wessel" in silver letters: your immortal name. As *Sturmführer*, you march in front of the young Fascists in our allied Italy, to whom their leader pinned your immortal name on their eagle shield.

Horst Wessel, you worker, you marched with us on that May 1st of 1933, on that day of German labor. You marched with us in the endless procession among them, working with their heads and hands, who had come together through your example, who wanted to honor and love German labor again. You will continue to walk ahead of them, to show them the national community, you worker Horst Wessel.

Horst Wessel, you student, you conquered the youth of the universities with the swastika. They stood up against everything alien and un-German. They handed over dirt and trash to the flames. You showed them how to defend themselves instead of blind knowledge from books, cheerfulness and hope instead of a bleak view of the future. You live among them as a German student.

Horst Wessel, you singer! Never in the Third Reich will your victorious song perish. It has become the consecration song of the whole nation. The brown and black and gray columns stand in solemn posture at the sound of it. Every act of consecration closes with your song as a vow. The flags are lowered at the open grave of those who have gathered for your storm of the dead, until your song calls out to them: "Raise the flag!" Immortal you are, like your shining image Theodor Körner, the student, singer, and freedom fighter!

Horst Wessel, you German! Your name rings immortal in German regions over which the sun symbol of the swastika now shines. Everywhere in the German fatherland squares, streets, and buildings bear your name. You have regained the capital of Germany through your struggle and death, and in the middle of German Berlin, in the Nikolai cemetery, you rest, having passed through storm and struggle to immortality. Your grave has become a place of pilgrimage for young and old; the flowers on it never fade. You have reawakened in German youth the spirit of the German fighters of Langemark, the spirit of fortitude, devotion, and loyalty. Horst Wessel, you fulfilled the words of a German workers' poet: "Germany must live, even if we must die!"

ENJOYED THIS BOOK?

TO READ MORE, VISIT US AT

ANTELOPEHILLPUBLISHING.COM

www.ingramcontent.com/pod-product-compliance
Lightning Source LLC
Chambersburg PA
CBHW031502120626
46545CB00005B/1710